"If ever you sho[...] be ignited, your sou[...] you've always wanted with God. This book is a treasure in my personal library that will continue to get underlined and tattered as I refer to it for years to come."

—LYSA TERKEURST, president of Proverbs 31 Ministries, national speaker, and author of *What Happens When Women Say Yes to God*

"We all know there is power in prayer, but it's not always easy to exercise that power. Terry Glaspey's *25 Keys to Life-Changing Prayer* provides deep insights into how to pray and pray effectively in the power of God's Spirit. This book is an excellent guide for making prayer your everyday practice."

—JOSH MCDOWELL, author of *More Than a Carpenter*

"We all need to be inspired to pray more, and Terry Glaspey's book on prayer does just that. It is delightfully written and entertaining to read. I have known Terry for many years and have seen that he has the talent of a true writer. He also has a heart that longs for a closer walk with God and the assurance that his life is being lived in an effective and fruitful way. And he knows that none of this happens without prayer."

—STORMIE OMARTIAN, author of The Power of a Praying® series

"Writing with the winsome tone of an encouraging friend, Terry Glaspey uses a little book to explore a big topic: the often daunting challenge of prayer. *25 Keys to Life-Changing Prayer* is the perfect primer for someone new to prayer, and great inspiration for someone who desires to renew their prayers."

—GARY THOMAS, author of *Sacred Marriage* and founder of the Center for Evangelical Spirituality

"Prayer has long been a mystifying, challenging, and laborsome process for me, but *25 Keys to Life-Changing Prayer* is like a lifeline. It is penetrating, concise, and uncommonly practical. Glaspey gives believers all the tools we need to cultivate a life of prayer. Read it. Apply it. And enjoy stepping into the presence of God."

—**JEFF CROSBY**, editor and compiler of
Days of Grace Through the Year

"Terry Glaspey's *25 Keys to Life-Changing Prayer* unlocks the heart and opens the door to welcoming God's presence into our lives moment-by-moment. Glaspey shows us that prayer is not about religious ritual but about a familiar friendship with God. This book is filled with simple yet profound steps that will help every reader move toward a more intimate relationship with God and begin to see the world through His eyes every minute of every day."

—**SHARON JAYNES**, international speaker and
author of *Becoming a Woman who Listens to God*

"I've read quite a few books on prayer—from classic to contemporary—and this is the most practical and winsome book on prayer I've ever read. Rather than coming at me like a saint from the past whose prayer life and prayers are way outside my grasp, Terry Glaspey comes alongside and nudges me along, providing useful suggestions and illustrations that encourage me to be a much more purposeful and regular pray-er. How did he know I need this right now?"

—**STAN JANTZ** is CEO of ConversantLife.com
and coauthor of *Growing as a Christian 101*

25 Keys to Life-Changing Prayer

TERRY GLASPEY

HARVEST HOUSE PUBLISHERS

EUGENE, OREGON

Cover design by e210 Design, Eagan, Minnesota

Cover photo © iStockphoto / drflet

25 Keys to Life-Changing Prayer
Copyright © 2010 by Terry Glaspey
Published by Harvest House Publishers
Eugene, Oregon 97402
www.harvesthousepublishers.com

ISBN 978-0-7369-2672-0

Printed in the United States of America

12 13 14 15 16 / BP-SK / 10 9 8 7 6 5 4 3 2

Contents

Introduction

This is a little book about a large topic...prayer.

In one sense, prayer is one of the simplest things we can do—we are invited to just open our hearts and open our mouths, and talk to God.

A child can pray.

In another sense, prayer is one of the hardest things to do. Most people struggle with their prayers from time to time, often feeling them to be inadequate or irrelevant or foolish or ineffective. Prayer can seem like a strange and pointless endeavor. If prayer is a conversation, it is a conversation with someone we can't see and we can't hear...at least not with our eyes and ears. And it requires faith and discipline to have an effective prayer life. The greatest saints spent their whole lives learning how to pray.

Yes, prayer is a simple idea. But it is not a simple practice.

If we are honest, the vast majority of us don't pray very much, very often, or with any strong sense that our prayers really matter or make any difference. We might say a prayer over our meal or intone an "amen" at the conclusion of a prayer during the church service. If something awful happens—or we fear it might—we breathe a quick prayer, almost like a lucky charm against the danger. Other than that, we may manage to squeeze in a few moments for prayer every day, but all too often our prayers feel unfocused and the actual experience of praying sometimes seems (dare we admit it?) boring and pointless. It may be a nice little religious ritual, but we aren't sure it actually accomplishes anything.

Prayer can seem like one of the hardest parts of our spiritual life.

———————

That's where this little book comes in. It is born out of my struggle to learn how to pray more effectively and to get myself to actually pray instead of just talking about it. I can't offer any magic formula that will make prayer easier—it always requires some discipline and commitment—but I can share with you some of the things that have jump-started my prayer life and helped me to be both more consistent and more excited about praying. In this book we'll explore 25 keys to expanding, improving, and energizing your prayer life. If you try to make these part of your own prayer experience, you'll find them life-changing. None of them are extremely difficult, and all of them will make a difference.

These chapters contain some of the insights and disciplines that I have learned along my fumbling pathway to becoming a better prayer. They are the result of much study of what the Bible has to teach us about prayer, the read-

When you come right down to it, prayer is ultimately not something you can learn from a book.

ing of a lot of classic and contemporary books on the subject, and, perhaps more than anything else, what I have learned from my own experience with prayer.

When you come right down to it, prayer is ultimately not something you can learn from a book. But before you decide to take this book back to the store to get a refund, let me explain...

The knowledge you can get by reading about prayer is not useless, but it will take you only so far. A book on prayer can teach you some of the principles and theology that undergird prayer. It can share with you some of the methods and practices that have helped people learn to pray regularly and powerfully. But in the end, we learn best by doing. You cannot read a book of golf tips and conclude that you'll immediately be able to play like a professional or read a cookbook and automatically be able to cook like Julia Child. Neither can you read a sex manual and think that by the knowledge you've attained you'll automatically be able to please your spouse. Knowledge is good and important. But in itself it isn't enough. Some things have to be learned through practice.

———

So what I'm asking you to do as you read this little book is to not only consider the insights and practice I'm going to share with you, but to actually try them out. I remember some of the difficulties I had with my science textbooks in school. I would diligently pour over their pages in quest of an understanding of the fundamentals of physics or chemistry, or more truthfully, just enough knowledge to pass the upcoming exam. But all too often, after finishing the assigned chapters, I would still be left scratching my head, not quite sure if I got the point. Thankfully these readings were usually followed by lab time, where we performed experiments based on what we had read. It was usually during these hands-on experiments that I had my "aha" moments. When I performed the experiments, the principles taught in the textbooks came to life.

Learning about prayer is much like that. If this little book succeeds in energizing your prayer life, it will be because you have spent at least twice the time you spent reading about prayer in actually praying. So join with me, a chapter at a time, in exploring some concepts and practices that will reignite your desire to pray.

1

Remember That Prayer Is More About Relationship Than Ritual

When I was a child I would kneel down by my bed every evening, fold my hands together, and "say my prayers." I don't know that I ever expected them to be answered very specifically, but I understood it as part of my duty. I was a Christian and praying was something Christians did. God seemed pretty distant to me at that time, but I wanted to keep Him happy by performing the nightly ritual of reciting "Now I lay me down to sleep," and then, when I got older, the Lord's Prayer.

During my junior high years I began to read the Bible for myself and listen to the stories and testimonies of those who seemed to know God more intimately than I did. I began to understand that God was not a far-off unapproachable deity, but Someone who cared about me, the struggles of my life, and my hopes and dreams. I learned that God was not only powerful but personal. Not an abstract power to be placated by my adherence to little rituals—such as "saying my prayers"—but Someone who loved me and I could lean upon. This awareness began to change the way I thought about prayer. Prayer was no longer a ritual to be performed; it was true communication. I could actually talk with God, and He would listen. And often, in my heart of hearts, I could sense the whisper of an answer.

Understanding that God wants to commune with us and to communicate with us—to be present in our lives (hang with us, if you will) and to have an ongoing conversation—is the foundation upon which prayer is based.

————

Some people treat prayer like a formality, and though God hears those prayers, they are unlikely to lead to deeper intimacy with Him. Others see prayer more as a magic formula they can use to solve all their problems, a secret recipe for getting God's help to fulfill their needs and desires. They call on God as though He is their servant and they can—if they use the right words—get Him to serve their bidding. It's as though He were a vending machine ready to dispense whatever they desire. That is certainly not what prayer is designed to be.

Some books on prayer would lead us to believe it is all about saying just the right words—as though God acts on our behalf only when we punch in the correct password. As Groucho Marx used to say on his game show: "Say the magic word, the duck comes down, and you win a hundred dollars."

Prayer is what transforms religion into relationship.

Nor is prayer a magic wand that we can wave over every situation and expect the desired results. Instead, prayer is all about relationship with God. It is the natural response that comes from experiencing intimacy with Him. At its heart, prayer is primarily two things: *communion* and *communication*. It is both the practice of welcoming God's presence into our lives and the practice of speaking with Him about all the many concerns in our lives.

Prayer is the beating heart of the spiritual life. It is impossible to imagine spiritual growth without the practice of prayer. Prayer is what transforms religion into relationship. With prayer our faith no longer consists of lofty thoughts and philosophies and doctrines *about* God, but becomes the basis for a friendship *with* God. In prayer we experience the depth of that friendship, whether through spending quiet moments with Him or by opening our heart and communicating the deepest things we think and feel.

The goal of our communion with God in prayer is to become aware of His presence, a presence that is always with us. It means keeping company with Him, moment by moment as we go through our days, practicing the awareness of His reality in our lives. As we will explore in a later chapter, it is the art of "practicing the presence of God."

Our communication with God should be more like talking things over with a dear friend than performing a ritual or fulfilling a duty. Prayer is not a philosophical monologue or some kind of self-talk by which we work out our problems. Nor is it a religious exercise we perform in order to gain points or favor with God. It is not an address to an unknowable and impersonal Creator-Being, but communication with a loving heavenly Father. That is why the model prayer Jesus gave His disciples, when they asked Him how to pray, begins: "Our Father."

We enter into this intimate relationship with God by accepting what Jesus has done on our behalf. Through our relationship with Him we can draw close to the heavenly Father. In Jesus Christ we "may approach God with freedom and confidence" (Ephesians 3:12). The message of the Christian gospel is that God reached down to the human race in the person of Jesus Christ, who came to live and die as one of us, to experience the fullness of our human experiences, and to provide a new destiny for humanity. In the Old Testament Scriptures, a priest would represent the people before God. But now Jesus has become our representative, a high priest whose actions make it possible for us to have direct access to God. As Hebrews 4:14-16 reminds us:

> Therefore, since we have a great high priest who has gone through the heavens, Jesus the Son of God, let us hold firmly to the faith we profess. For we do not have a high priest who is unable to sympathize with our weaknesses, but we have one who has been tempted in every way, just as we are—yet was without sin. Let us then approach the throne of grace with confidence, so that we may receive mercy and find grace to help us in our time of need.

But our help doesn't end there. For God has given us His Holy Spirit, resident within us, to lead and guide us into the life that God has for us. One of the powerful ways He helps us is through prayer. When we wonder what we should pray about, we are promised the help of the Holy Spirit:

> The Spirit helps us in our weakness. We do not know what we ought to pray for, but the Spirit

himself intercedes for us with groans that words cannot express. And he who searches our hearts knows the mind of the Spirit, because the Spirit intercedes for the saints in accordance with God's will (Romans 8:26)

Our intimacy with God is Trinitarian in nature—the Father who loves us, the Son who intercedes for us, and the Holy Spirit who leads and guides us. All this is based upon the intimacy of our relationship with God. He has come near to us, and is still near to us—as near as the breath we draw to form a prayer on our lips.

In our prayers we expose our true selves to God. Vulnerability is a hard thing for most of us, but it is safe to be vulnerable with Him. We can share everything that is on our hearts: fears, worries, guilt, aspirations, desires, and needs. And God bestows upon us the dignity of listening to everything we say—no matter how foolish, self-centered, and self-indulgent it might be. He hears us, and He cares. And He not only hears, but He speaks. Into the quietness of our hearts He speaks words of hope and peace and comfort to keep us going, or words of challenge and correction to set us on a better path.

The purpose of the communication we experience in prayer is like that in any other relationship—not to extract something from the other person but to get to know them and to allow them to get to know us. We cannot truly call someone our friend until we have been willing to be vulnerable and to reveal our deepest and truest self to them, with all its faults and foibles. Similarly, true prayer is the great act of vulnerability. If prayer is only a religious nicety, then it will contribute little to our spiritual growth. But if it is the way we know and are known, then it is the key to the spiritual life and holds the promise of changing our lives.

2

Deepen Your Understanding
of God's Strength and Love

Why pray?

The reason we can pray is that we are not alone.

Life can often be difficult and challenging, and we can feel so hopeless. We can be confused, worried, or at the end of our rope. We can feel that no one understands our struggles, our questions, our confusions, or our pain. Sometimes our problems seem so complicated or embarrassing that we just don't know who we can talk to. In such times we feel completely alone, as though we walk through this shadowed valley a stranger to the rest of humanity. And this sense of being alone only multiplies the hardship.

But the invitation to pray reminds us that we don't have to walk through our difficulties alone.

When we reach the end of our rope, have exerted

ourselves to the fullest extent, and even felt tempted to simply give up, we are reminded that we are not alone, nor are we abandoned to our own resources. God is both caring and responsive, and He will meet with us in prayer. There is One who listens. One who understands and cares. God is with us. God hears us. His ear is available to us. His strength is present when we don't feel strong, when we don't feel that we can go on.

Our prayers are like rescue flares, shot into the black nothingness of our fear and pain, that bring close the One who can guide us through the darkness and hopelessness and fright. Of course, He is there even before we pray, because He is always with us. But when we open our hearts and our mouths to pray, we are reminded of that Presence.

"Never will I leave you; never will I forsake you," the Lord has promised (Hebrews 13:5).

Prayer is like the midnight phone call we make to a trusted friend, where even the sound of that person's voice is enough to begin to calm us down, to give us perspective, to provide us hope. But the friend we call out to in prayer is the Friend who knows us more intimately than any human friend could possibly know us, the Friend who has resources of strength that no human friend could possibly have, and the Friend who loves us more deeply and completely than we could ever be loved by any human person.

In prayer we find the therapy and healing and relationship that come from being heard. Then hope and faith can be reborn in our hearts. The invitation to pray is an invitation to communicate with God, to pour out all the hurt in our lives to Him. The great promise of prayer is that God hears these cries.

"Never will I leave you; never will I forsake you," the Lord has promised (HEBREWS 13:5).

Prayer also reminds us that we are not limited to our own resources. How hopeless life would often feel if that were the case. But I have learned time and again that although my resources are limited, His resources are limitless.

As the psalmist writes, "God is our refuge and strength, an ever-present help in trouble" (Psalm 46:1).

In the troubled times of my life, when life has felt overwhelming and difficult, I have learned that God is easy to talk with. He cares about me: about my struggles, my doubts, my worries, my sense of failure, my hopes and dreams and desires. The amazing reality of prayer is that the God who created the whole universe is Someone who wants to relate to me, to walk with me through the joy and confusion of my days, to comfort me in the dark hours, to challenge me when I make the wrong decisions, and to strengthen me to make better ones.

Our prayers are a request for God's intervention in our lives. Praying is the act of inviting Him into the situations that we face and the needs that we have.

We pray because we are not alone.

3

Recognize the Amazing Power of Prayer

What if I told you that I had discovered an amazing diet secret—a simple way that you could lose weight quickly and permanently? You'd be skeptical, right? You might be a little bit curious to hear what I had to say, but cynical that I could tell you something you hadn't heard before. You'd probably think something like this: *I've tried a lot of different diets. Nothing has worked for me. Diets don't work.* But in dismissing it too quickly you might just miss out on an opportunity to change your life.

So it is with prayer. Perhaps because of the way we were raised or because of disappointing experiences with prayer, we often do not see it for the powerful tool that it is. Prayer is not merely a religious nicety meant to be taken lightly; it is a dangerous, earth-shattering

act, the powerful engine that God uses to accomplish
His will on this earth.

———

The realization that God uses our feeble prayers to
accomplish His will should fill us with awe and wonder.
How astonishing that He chooses to use the prayers of
His children to make things happen in both the earthly
and heavenly realms. Prayer is powerful! Through prayer,
souls are brought into God's kingdom, lives changed,
and miracles performed. And our humble prayers are
what God uses to do all this. Tertullian, one of the early
church fathers, reminds us of this awesome power:

> Prayer has been known to recall the souls of the
> departed from the very path of death, to trans-
> form the weak, to restore the sick, to purge the
> possessed, to open prison-bars, to loose the
> bonds of the innocent. Likewise it washes away
> faults, repels temptations, extinguishes persecu-
> tions, consoles the fainthearted, cheers the high-
> spirited, escorts travelers, appeases waves, makes
> robbers stand aghast, nourishes the poor, gov-
> erns the rich, upraises the fallen, arrests the fall-
> ing, confirms the standing.

But the power of prayer is not limited to the more
spectacular miracles it sometimes brings about. Perhaps

it can be seen even more in the greatest miracle it brings about—the transformation of our hearts and minds and souls. I have seen it in my own life and in the lives of others—finding the strength to put away deeply held prejudices, to conquer addictions, and to overcome long-ingrained bad habits. I know that prayer changes people because I have witnessed it firsthand, radical transformations inexplicable except for the intervention of God.

Prayer is as necessary to our spiritual health as exercise is to our bodily health.

But if prayer is so powerful, why don't we embrace it more often and more readily? It is usually not hard to convince us to spend time on things that we deem to be truly important. We rarely need, for example, to be lectured on the necessity of eating or sleeping. But some things we know to be important are not as easy to convince ourselves to do, such as getting adequate exercise. We struggle to find the time to work out even though we know that our bodies need regular exertion to maintain our health. Prayer is as necessary to our spiritual health as exercise is to our bodily health. But we still seem to need to be constantly reminded.

You might find it helpful to keep a record of your

answered prayers as a reminder of the effectiveness of prayer. As you hear of a need or experience one yourself, you can jot it down in a notebook, along with the date. You can use such a notebook as a running list of things to pray about, and it is useful for reference when you spend an extended time in prayer. You will discover in keeping such a record that many of your prayers get specific, and sometimes miraculous, answers. Some answers come quickly; others take time. But if you keep track of them, you will likely be surprised at the frequency of the answers. We tend to forget so quickly when God has acted on our behalf, or we dream up other explanations for the answers we get, but a notebook of answered prayers can be a permanent reminder of what God has done for us. Keeping a record of these answers can be a great faith-building exercise in reminding you of the power of prayer.

4

Learn That the Best Way to Learn to Pray Is by Praying

On hearing that I was writing a book about prayer, a friend inquired whether I believed there was a secret to prayer. My first inclination was to say "heavens, no." Finding purpose in prayer is not a matter of learning some secret technique or magical set of words.

But then I thought better of my answer.

For yes, there is one great secret to prayer.

But I think my friend found the answer I gave him to be a letdown. For in my experience, the secret of prayer is...*wait for it*...to pray.

You are never going to learn to pray except by praying. No matter how many books (however good they may be) you might read, no matter how much you think deeply about the meaning of prayer or how much good advice you might gather, no matter how much you study what the Bible says about prayer, you'll never learn how to pray without actually praying. Prayer is one of those things that must be learned by doing.

From time to time, as you make your way through this little book, I hope you will find something fresh and new that will inspire you to pray, to practice what I am preaching. When that happens, I hope it will not just be a moment when you stroke your chin, wrinkle your brow, and think deep thoughts about prayer. I hope you will set the book down and actually pray.

In fact, why not take a moment right now to speak with God?

5

Pray Boldly

Jesus made some incredible statements about the efficacy of prayer:

"Therefore I tell you, whatever you ask for in prayer, believe that you have received it, and it will be yours" (Mark 11:24)

"And I will do whatever you ask in my name, so that the Son may bring glory to the Father. You may ask for anything in my name, and I will do it" (John 14:13-14).

And yet, despite these promises, many Christians have become discouraged about prayer and maybe a little tentative when it comes to asking God for anything specific. These statements by Jesus are wonderful promises...but they are also hard for us to believe. They don't exactly square up with most of our experiences in prayer. We have prayed, but we have not always seen the kind of amazing results Jesus is talking about. The mountains didn't move, which sometimes makes the

mountains seem that much steeper to climb. Perhaps
such experiences have caused you to become discouraged with prayer or to reduce the subject of your praying to safe pious niceties. Perhaps you have come to the
place where you don't expect much out of your prayers.
Or maybe, because you are afraid of failing to get the
answers you want, and perhaps because you're afraid
that your faith will be shaken if you make another request that is not met, you mostly just quit asking. After
all, the one sure cure for avoiding disappointment in
prayer is to not pray. So you lose a sense of boldness in
bringing your needs to God and limit yourself to safe
prayers that don't require an answer.

———

But there are other ways that you can lose your boldness. Perhaps you're afraid to pray boldly because you
aren't certain that what you are praying for is the will
of God. Unfortunately, it can be difficult to ascertain
God's will with absolute certainty, so perhaps you think
it's easier not to pray about the matter at hand—just to
be on the safe side.

Or maybe, in your heart of hearts, you are kept from
praying because you don't really—in the deepest part of
your soul—actually believe that God is all that concerned
with you or your problems. *After all*, you might say, *the
God who is in charge of keeping the whole universe running*

smoothly has a lot more to be concerned about than me and my comparatively trivial problems, right? You may even believe that it is wrong to bother God with your little wish list or your personal struggles when other people are struggling with more significant issues and we live in a world wracked by poverty, war, death, and suffering. It might not feel appropriate to pray about your sprained ankle when you know that children in other countries are dying of malnutrition or soldiers are in grave danger fighting overseas.

> *He wants us to come to Him with all our needs and desires...and even our uncertainties.*

And so, many of us fail to pray with boldness. We settle for timid, safe prayers that don't ask much from God. Whether this attitude is caused by our disappointments or our fear of further disappointments, or whether it is caused by our uncertainty about God's will or by our desire not to ask more of God than we should—we can easily lose a sense of boldness in prayer.

Yet there are still those statements from Jesus that we can't ignore, statements that indicate that prayer—even bold and outrageous prayer—is always acceptable to God. He wants us to come to Him with all our needs and desires...and even our uncertainties. We

won't always get what we want when we pray, but
it is always within God's will that we ask. He loves
us so much that it is always appropriate to ask. We
don't have to agonize over whether we should pray
about anything. We should just pray. We can ask
boldly and with expectancy, and
then be willing to accept an answer other than yes if it comes.

*He wants us to
discover that ultimately
He, in Himself, is
the best answer to
all our prayers.*

God wants us to experience
the intimacy of relationship with
Him that comes through prayer.
That intimacy allows us to be
bold in our asking. Such bold
asking is even desirable as it is a
good reminder that we need to always rely on Him. So
ask boldly. We may not always receive what we are hoping for, but He wants us to discover that ultimately He,
in Himself, is the best answer to all our prayers. We
don't so much pray to receive an answer as to receive
His answer. I am reminded of a wonderful quote from
George MacDonald:

> What if the main object in God's idea of prayer be
> the supplying of our great, endless need—the need
> of Himself? What if the good of all our smaller
> and lower needs lies in this, that they help to drive
> us to God? Hunger may drive the runaway child

home, and he may or may not be fed at once, but he needs his mother more than his dinner.

So pray boldly. Pray expectantly. But then be ready to accept the final answer when it comes, knowing that He knows what is best for our ultimate good.

6

Overcome a
Naturalistic Mindset

Recently I prayed for a friend whose body was riddled with cancer. The doctors gave him no chance to survive beyond a couple of months. His situation was dire and beyond the hope of medicine. But even though I felt a little foolhardy about it, I joined with many others in praying for him.

Sometimes when I pray for what can only be described as a miracle, for something out of the ordinary, I struggle with feeling a little bit silly about it. Even though I should know better, I can easily get caught up in the thinking of my culture and question the rationality of my prayers. I want to have strong faith, but I am influenced by the secularist mindset of my culture. As a rational person is it reasonable for me to believe that

God actually gets involved in human needs and human problems? Or is that just an outdated, premodern way of thinking?

It can be hard for us to believe in the supernatural when we live in a culture where science and psychology seem to have an explanation for everything. We know why people get sick and what makes their body heal itself. We understand how weather patterns work (at least in general, though we still don't trust the weather reports). We have medicines to cure the sick and psychological therapies to restore the emotionally disturbed. We grasp the consequences of poor decisions, and we understand how certain pathologies can assert themselves in the form of religious manias or obsessions. And if we try hard enough, we can usually come up with a rational explanation for even the most miraculous occurrence.

In trying to explain, though, we sometimes explain away—we eliminate the mystery of life in our attempt to reduce it to a scientific equation. This kind of thinking, called *naturalism*, rejects the reality of the supernatural, believing instead that the only things that are real are the things we can experience with our senses. If we can't see, hear, or touch it, then it doesn't exist. The spiritual world is not only unnecessary, but it is also not real.

Such a way of thinking reduces our life experiences to only the physical realm, and it ends up dismissing some of the deepest and most mysterious realities of our lives. For example, how do you explain that you are deeply and passionately in love with another person? Is that just the result of a particular chemical coursing through your bloodstream? Is it a psychological projection of your self-love onto another being? Or is it just a Darwinian response to the need for the species to propagate? Can anyone who has actually been in love be satisfied with such answers? There may be some truth in each of these explanations—up to a point. But none of them really answer to the fullness of the reality we experience when we are in love. And it is that way with many of the most important things in life.

Most Christians quickly reject a naturalistic philosophy since they believe that God exists in a realm outside the merely physical. But perhaps sometimes, deep down, we have been so deeply affected by this supposedly scientific way of looking at things that we are suspicious of anything outside our immediate experience. It is hard for us to believe in divine intervention. We might feel foolish praying for a miracle since miracles are unscientific. It can be easy for us to become "functional atheists," those who give lip service to the reality of God but don't really expect or believe in His ability or desire to intervene in our lives. Even if we don't buy into the naturalistic mindset, we may still have low expectations when it comes to anything outside our normal experience.

There is more at work than meets the eye or that can be examined in a microscope or be viewed in a telescope.

For the Christian, there is both a physical and a spiritual reality. And sometimes the two are interconnected. It doesn't have to be one or the other. If you are sick, you should see a doctor. But you should also pray. There is both a physical and a spiritual element to so many of our experiences. As one of Shakespeare's characters says in the face of a reductionistic frame of mind: "There are more things in heaven and earth, Horatio, than are dreamt of in your philosophy" (*Macbeth*, Act 1, Scene 5).

We should never be afraid of embracing the mystery of faith and the mystery of prayer. Although we don't want to be childish or immature, sometimes it is appropriate to pray even when your request might feel irrational (remember that Jesus spoke of "moving mountains") or when that request could just as well be answered by purely human means. We should still pray.

We should not accept a diminished view of the world or reject the mystery of the supernatural. The best way to remind us that the naturalistic worldview is inadequate is by keeping up a vital prayer life. It creates a vivid reminder that there is more at work than meets the eye or that can be examined in a microscope or be viewed in a telescope. There is an awesome power above and behind the world, at work in a realm parallel to ours that has an effect on the world we live in.

Despite the doctor's best medical knowledge, the friend I mentioned at the beginning of this chapter experienced a miracle. For no reason that could be scientifically or medically adduced, his cancer went into remission. He has lived many years beyond the doctor's prediction. In retrospect I realized I shouldn't feel so foolish about asking for a miracle.

7

Don't Worry About
Your Feelings—Just Pray

When I first began writing books, I labored under an illusion about what it was like to write. I thought of writing as a kind of magical process where an author experiences bursts of creative inspiration and the words just come flooding out onto the page. I assumed, therefore, that the best time to write was when I felt inspired. I thought that if I just waited, the great creative muse would descend upon me, and I could pour forth great sentences—sentences filled with interesting ideas, delivered in a polished style. Sometimes I would sit in front of the computer and just stare at the screen, waiting for it to happen. When it didn't, I would put off the writing or play a game or two of solitaire while I waited to feel inspired enough to get started. The result was that I didn't get a lot of writing done, but I got really good at solitaire.

Once in a while, I would indeed feel tremendously inspired, and my fingers would race across the keyboard, trying to keep up with my insights. Problem was, when I reread this "inspired" writing a couple days later, I often discovered that it wasn't particularly good. Sometimes it even ended up in the wastebasket.

I have learned that my best writing is more about discipline and hard work than waiting for inspiration. Some of my best writing actually happens when I don't feel particularly inspired. I have discovered that the *feeling* of being inspired is highly overrated. What is more important is to be disciplined enough to plant myself in my chair in front of my computer and get to work. Usually a sense of being inspired comes *after* I have started to slog away at the project I'm working on.

It is the same with prayer. If I wait to feel like praying, I find that I don't pray much. But if I make prayer a habit, then I am often surprised with the wonderful experiences I have in talking with God—even when I didn't really feel like praying.

———

Sometimes we may be tempted to wait until we feel spiritually centered and at peace before we are ready to pray. We forget that it is when we are off-balance, confused, frustrated, angry, disappointed, or under temptation that we most need to seek God's presence. Our

emotions are so changeable and undependable. I can
sometimes be having a perfectly wonderful day when
the silliest little thing can send me
into an emotional tailspin. All it
can take is an unkind or thoughtless comment, an unexpected in-
convenience, or having a little
accident, like a cup of coffee
spilled on my desk, and then I
don't feel as happy as I did. Or

*He is not looking
for us to have beautiful,
holy, and pious feelings
before we pray.*

maybe I didn't get enough sleep or exercise, and so I feel
lethargic and depressed. Sometimes it doesn't take anything significant to happen to me and I just don't feel at
all like praying...or doing anything spiritual.

Maybe our problem is our belief that God wants
us to get all our bad attitudes and negative emotions
in check before we pray. That He wants us to get our
niceness in order before we do something spiritual like
praying. Otherwise we are being hypocritical, right?

Well, I think this kind of thinking comes from a
wrong perspective of prayer. If prayer is an intimate
and honest conversation, it means that we can bring all
our junk with us into that conversation. A true friend
is someone who sees the worst of you and still loves
you and wants to talk with you. Our Truest Friend is

the God who loves us and wants us to come as we are in prayer. He is not looking for us to have beautiful, holy, and pious feelings before we pray. He is looking for honesty, authenticity, and humility. He invites us to come as we are. Maybe we can manage only a weak and halfhearted prayer. Well, that is better than not praying. Even the weakest and feeblest prayer will bring us closer to God than the most exalted ruminations on theology.

———

If we wait until we feel like praying, our praying will be as sporadic and undependable as our emotional states. That is why it's important to develop a habit of praying. Perhaps you can start by thinking about some obvious times during the day that you could begin to pray regularly.

A good start might be the first thing in the morning, before you climb out of bed. When my alarm goes off, I try, no matter how tired, to pray a quick prayer along these lines: "Lord, before my feet touch the floor this morning, I want to offer my day to You. Use me as You will this day to be a blessing to others. Use me as a vessel through which Your love can flow. Help me to keep my heart set upon Your ways, and let my priorities today be Your priorities. Lead and guide me this day. Amen."

Or in the evening, you might think through your

day as you lie down to sleep. Instead of being overwhelmed by your worries, you can offer them to God
and ask for His help and wisdom to do what needs to
be done. You can ask forgiveness for the times during
the day when you were thoughtless, rude, unkind, and
selfish, maybe making a mental note to set some things
right during the day that follows. You can ask for a rest-
ful sleep and to experience the peace that passes understanding.

For me, lunchtime is a good time to pray, as I usually spend my lunch hour alone. I offer thanks for the
food I am eating, but beyond that I use it as a moment
to acknowledge God's goodness, unburden myself of
some concerns, and seek an intimate moment to experience His love and grace.

Everyone probably will find different times that
work best for them. What is important is just to get in
the habit of doing it. Think through your daily schedule
and figure out when the best times might be to regularly
talk with God. Then start establishing the habit. Once
you establish a habit of seeking Him every day, then it
doesn't matter so much whether you feel like praying.
You just do it anyway. And no matter how uninspired
or unspiritual we might feel, He meets with us in prayer.
Someone once said that the secret to writing is just show-
ing up. Perhaps that is the secret to prayer as well.

8

Pray Honestly

If you are like me, sometimes you may feel uncomfortable or embarrassed talking to God because you know your life is not what it should be. None of us feel adequate or morally pure enough to be in God's presence. We feel like failures, like hypocrites. And if we are honest with ourselves, we are likely all of these things. But that need not, and should not, keep us from praying.

"Give up trying to look like a saint," Brennan Manning's spiritual director once told him. "It'll be a lot better for everybody." This is a great reminder for me when I begin to think my prayers are valuable to God only after I've got my act together. I need to be reminded that being a follower of Jesus is not a matter of polishing myself up to make myself more presentable to God; it's a matter of being honest about how far I fall short of being the person I know I should be and reaching out to accept the freely given, wild, and untamed grace of God.

We can come as we are. His desire for us is not based on our performance. If we grasp this truth—really believe it—it will change the way we think about prayer.

———

I still have a little picture that one of my daughters drew for me when she was small. She had dumped out her box of crayons on the floor and carefully chosen the colors she wanted to use to draw a picture that she described as "a man, a house, and a doggie." I was glad for the description since the picture was made up primarily of great spiraling loops, urgent cross-hatchings, and squiggles of various colors. The drawing would not have won any awards for its artistic creativity or been chosen to hang in any museum or gallery. But I loved it. It was precious to me because it was created *for* me—a gift of the heart from my sweet daughter.

I am convinced that God feels the same way about our faltering, fumbling, imperfect prayers. In God's eyes, any prayer that is honest and authentic is precious to Him. This gives me the freedom to express everything that is inside me. For I know He loves me…and He loves even my looping scrawls of crayoned passion. I'm glad I don't always have to color inside the lines, because my hand and heart are rarely that steady.

Sometimes my prayers are carefully thought out, each word painstakingly chosen. Occasionally, I'll sit down and write out my prayers, trying to express as clearly as I can the depths of what is in my heart. I'll work and rework each phrase, crafting it like a poem, trying to capture the rhythm of my soul's cries in the dance of the words, trying—always imperfectly—to make them say exactly what I mean, to capture precisely what I want to express to God. This has an amazing way of focusing my mind on what matters most. And the process of pouring out my heart on paper becomes a prayer in itself.

Most of the time, though, my prayers are less articulate. They arise out of the difficulties and struggles of my life—they are mostly cries and groans filled with my pain and passion. They are not neat and tidy. They are not particularly religious. They are graffiti scrawled on the walls of heaven.

I've learned that anger and depression and frustration and confusion can give rise to prayers that are every bit as real and precious to God as any of my more devout outpourings. The psalms are filled with moments when David stands before God shaking an accusing finger at perceived injustices or forming words that barely conceal his feeling of abandonment. If there was anyone who might rightfully feel embarrassed about being honest with God, it would be David. After all, he was an adulterer and a murderer, a man of unbridled passion and overweening pride. He had failed God time and time again. If David, with all his checkered history, could speak so freely before God, then why not you and me?

I don't have to hide from God all the thoughts and feelings that aren't very pretty.

Like David, I don't have to hide from God all the thoughts and feelings that aren't very pretty. He is perfectly aware of what I am thinking and feeling. Why would I need to try to cloak my emotions in pious terms? In expressing myself freely and honestly, I usually come to understand more clearly the real nature of what is happening in my heart and soul. Recently, frustrated with what seemed like God's silence in the face of great pain in my life, I found myself saying these words through clenched teeth: "God, if You want You and me to have a good relationship, You're going to have to keep up Your end of the deal." I don't think I managed to shock Him with this little outburst. And once it was spoken aloud, it helped me to begin to uncover some of the ways I was trying to manipulate Him into changing my unpleasant circumstances.

The Old Testament is filled with examples of men and women who bargained with God. I think of Abraham, haggling with all the skill of a used-car salesman to convince God not to destroy Sodom. Or Jacob, wrestling with God and unwilling to give up until he has extracted a blessing. The prayer lives of these patriarchs are more reminiscent of the wheeling and dealing of a Middle Eastern street vendor than a polite and polished cleric. They give me hope that I can ask persistently, and even ask for the wrong things, knowing that God desires to hear my requests. One of Jesus' clearest teachings on prayer is that we should be bold to ask. That doesn't mean we'll always get what we want, but it does mean that the door is always open for our most heartfelt pleas to pass through.

I wonder if part of our problem is that we have made prayer into something unnatural, something that doesn't fit into our lives. We burden ourselves with guilt about a problem we can't figure out how to overcome, when the answer may rest in simply changing our perceptions. Maybe if we grasped prayer as something more natural—less as a religious ritual and more as a real conversation—it would be easier to pray. Prayer is not about pious thoughts and words; it is not about postures, techniques, or methods. It is less a matter of quality or quantity than passion.

Love is God's motivation for giving us the gift of prayer. God values the scrawls I make on the wall of heaven because He values me. I do not pray primarily to get the things I think I need or to fulfill a religious duty. I pray because God loves me and desires to be involved in my life. I pray because, however imperfectly and unfaithfully, I love Him and I desire His companionship with me on the journey that is my life. Prayer is the most intimate activity I can share with God, the utmost in self-revelation, the place where I can bare my heart and soul before Him. In prayer I am made vulnerable to God, my truest self is revealed, and I find the promise that God is transforming this ragamuffin into royalty—a child of the King.

9

Experiment with a Variety of Kinds of Prayer

What comes to mind when you hear or read the word *prayer*?

We have already said that prayer is essentially communion and communication. That seems simple enough.

But in another sense, prayer is complex and multifaceted. We tend to see prayer in a narrow and limited way. When we hear the word *prayer*, our mind jumps to one or two different kinds of prayer, failing to under stand that prayer encompasses so many different aspects of our walk with God. For the word *prayer* is used to talk about a variety of practices we can undertake to communicate with God. Many think of prayer as "asking God for something—either for our benefit or for the benefit of someone else." And while that is certainly one of the things we do when we pray, it falls far short of encompassing the many varied aspects of prayer.

Prayer can be supplication (asking for our own needs). Prayer can be intercession (praying for others). Prayer can be worship, confession of sins, contemplation, or practicing God's presence. There are lots of ways we should be praying if we are to have a balanced spiritual life.

———

Perhaps it would be helpful to think of prayer like a set of golf clubs. We need more than one club to be effective in playing the game of golf. As every golfer knows, there is one primary purpose in mind when we tee it up: to get that little white ball into the hole. But we use a number of different clubs to reach that goal: the driver, the woods, the irons, the pitching wedge, the sand wedge, and the putter. It all depends on the situation. During the playing of even a single hole, we will use a variety of different clubs, because each has a unique purpose and design. If we used our putter off the tee, we wouldn't be able to hit the ball very far. If we used our driver to hit the ball out of a sand trap—well, good luck. And a sand wedge is a poor choice for putting once we reach the green. Each club has its own use, but the whole set of clubs is necessary for success.

Likewise, any good cook can tell you how important it is to have a variety of tools when crafting a culinary delight. You need a variety of pots and pans, spatulas and whisks, to make a tasty dish. Heating water in a frying pan or trying to fluff up some eggs with a spatula just isn't very effective.

Since prayer is about relationship—our relationship with God—it has all the complexities of a relationship. We have lots of different kinds of conversations and encounters with our friends. It wouldn't be much of a friendship if we were always just asking them for stuff. Nor would it be a very meaningful relationship if we always talked to them but never listened. We'd think it a poor relationship if we never apologized when we failed or neglected them. And sometimes we don't even need to speak when we are with a dear friend. Just being in their presence, just being with them, is communication enough.

Prayer is made up of a variety of different forms and practices. The balanced prayer life will be one that partakes of each of them from time to time. Confession, petition, intercession, contemplation, worship, and others are all important aspects of prayer. They all achieve the goal of drawing us closer to God, but each operates in a different way. So if you have been thinking about prayer in a narrow and restricted way, I hope some of the chapters that follow will expand your thinking and equip you with different ways to connect with the One who loves us and longs to relate to us. When it comes to prayer, let's think bigger and broader. Let prayer become an adventure of discovery, of openness to learning new ways to connect with God.

10

Don't Be Afraid to Pray for Yourself and Your Needs

We all have many wants and needs, hopes and dreams, desires and passionate longings. And though we know from Scripture that God loves us and cares for us, we sometimes are reluctant to share our concerns with Him because we fear they're not important enough. In the grand scheme of things, some of our concerns may seem trivial, even to us, and therefore much too small for God to be bothered with. And so, sometimes we keep our needs to ourselves.

But we should never think that it is somehow more spiritual to suffer quietly, with only the assistance of our own limited resources, than to bring our needs and concerns before God. For He not only wants to give us the gift of eternal life, but also to provide us with what we need day-to-day. Sometimes our pride stands in the way. We must admit that we need Him and His intervention in our lives, and we should never be shy about asking for what we truly need. As Charles Spurgeon once wrote, "Asking is the rule of the Kingdom." Prayer isn't overcoming God's reluctance, but taking hold of His promises.

———

Jesus said, "Ask, and it will be given to you; seek and you will find; knock and the door will be opened to you. For everyone who asks receives; he who seeks finds; and to him who knocks, the door will be opened" (Luke 11:9-10). The image of seeking and knocking lets us know that sometimes we must be persistent in our praying and not just think that we have prayed once and can check it off our list. We should continue to pray until we receive an answer. Sometimes that answer might be *no* or *wait*, and sometimes that answer might take months or even years to come. But the answer will come.

Only pride keeps us from bringing our most deeply felt needs to our heavenly Father.

We should never be reluctant, once we have prayed for the needs of others, to turn our attention in prayer to our own needs. Jesus has invited us to ask for what we need. Remember the phrase from the Lord's Prayer: "Give us each day our daily bread" (Luke 11:3). There is nothing improper or unseemly about talking with God about the things that most concern us. Only pride keeps us from bringing our most deeply felt needs to our heavenly Father.

So what do you need right now? What are you concerned about? Perhaps this would be a good moment to talk with God about these very things.

11

Confess Your Sin

Life is a messy proposition. It is filled with choices, and I often make bad ones. My selfishness and carelessness sometimes hurt other people. I regularly say the wrong thing and do the wrong thing—even when I *know* it is the wrong thing. It's not that I don't try to be a good person—I care deeply about being the person God wants me to be—but even with my best intentions and mustering all my inner strength, my fallen self often prevails. And let's not try to pretty it up with any fancy evasions or psychological explanations. Let's call it what it is: *sin*.

Sometimes we may find ourselves hesitant to pray because of the state of our hearts and lives. Because we know that we live out our lives before an all-seeing God, it isn't surprising that we would feel shame and recognize our moral shortcomings when we approach Him in prayer. To make it worse, we know that not only our actions but even our thoughts are transparent to the

One who made us. In the brightness of God's holiness, all our evasions and imperfections become clear. The darkness of our self-deceptions must flee in the dawning of His light. And when we see ourselves as we really are, it may not be a pleasant experience. We know how far short we fall from being the kind of people we know we should be. We don't want to come to God with our mouths filled with requests while our hearts are filled with self-righteousness, evil imaginations, bitter emotions, and self-serving attitudes. Before we come to God in prayer, we want to be cleansed of our sin.

We come with all our imperfections, or we do not come at all.

But if we wait until we have our act together before we come to God, we will never be able to come. We come with all our imperfections, or we do not come at all.

The glorious truth about sin is that Jesus Christ has dealt with it. When we reach out to Him for forgiveness, He not only forgives the sins of our past, but also those still lurking in our future. Because of what He has done, we understand that sin doesn't have the power to separate us from God.

But while that is true, it is also true that you and I

continue to sin. And because He loves us, God wants us to be honest about these sins and to acknowledge and confess them. Here is the paradox: In Jesus we are already for given…and yet we are called to confess our sins. Our *experience* of forgiveness begins with asking. "If we confess our sins, he is faithful and just and will forgive our sins and purify us from all unrighteousness" (1 John 1:9).

Confession brings honesty and healing to our relationship with Him. Just as a hidden or unspoken wrong against one of my friends makes true communication with him or her almost impossible, so my refusal to come clean with God does damage to my ability to communicate freely and openly with Him. It isn't that He doesn't already know of my wrongdoing. Of course He knows. But it is critical for me to own up to the true state of my soul. As the psalmist acknowledges, "You know my folly, O God: my guilt is not hidden from you" (Psalm 69:5).

Sometimes we are reluctant to expose our shortcomings to the people in our lives for fear that they will stop loving and respecting us. But it is different with God. He already knows. And He knows that it is good for us to agree with Him about our true state. Solving any relationship problem usually begins with talking it out. In confession I can talk it out with God. I live in constant need of forgiveness. My acknowledgment of that fact is the beginning of the road to healing.

But that doesn't mean God wants me to punish myself with guilt. It means that He wants me to be honest about my sin and accept the forgiveness He offers. He doesn't call me to confession for His sake but for my sake. It is a necessity for my spiritual health.

The end result of confession is the knowledge that we are forgiven. This knowledge has two aspects: an *intellectual* awareness and an *experiential* awareness. Intellectually, it is a truth we can know beyond a shadow of a doubt. We are forgiven even when we do not feel forgiven. It is a reality based on God's love and what He has done for us in Christ. He has made the choice to forgive us.

Forgiveness also has an experiential element. When we have confidence that God has forgiven us, we will often experience that truth as a liberating emotion. We feel a great burden and weight lifted from our souls. We feel cleansed and know the joy of being able to start over. Again and again, God gives us the ability to reaffirm our commitment to Him and to start anew, with a clean slate, because He has forgiven us.

There is a heavy weight that comes with trying to hold onto our sins. As David prayed,

When I kept silent about my sin, my body
    wasted away
Through my groaning all day long.
For day and night Thy hand was heavy upon me;
My vitality was drained away as with the fever
    heat of summer.
I acknowledged my sin to You,
And my iniquity I did not hide;
I said, "I will confess my transgressions to the LORD";
And You forgave the guilt of my sin.

                (Psalm 32:3-5 NASB)

Because confession is so important for maintaining
an open and honest relationship with God, it should be
a part of the prayer life of every believer. Confession is a
great way to clear the air before we launch into making
requests. If I am going to spend some extended time
in prayer, I usually start with a few moments of honest self-searching and reflection. I've learned to let the
Holy Spirit bring to the surface any bitterness, resent-
ment, disobedience, or unhealthy emotions hiding in
the depths of my soul. As I become aware of each sin
in my life, I ask God to forgive me and help me walk
in a way that is more pleasing to Him. And then I consciously accept and embrace the forgiveness He has
already granted.

I don't worry about making sure I dredge up every
misdeed. There aren't enough hours in the day for that.

And God isn't withholding His love and forgiveness until we have vocalized every sin. It's not as though there is a balance sheet where every single sin must be balanced by a specific credit of forgiveness. No, He has forgiven us even before we ask. In fact, He forgave us even before we sinned. But confession is one of the keys to making our prayer life real and authentic; it's the doorway through which we should approach our loving Father.

12

Pray for Others

Many times when we pray, we build our requests around our needs. We come into God's presence with a shopping list of what we would like Him to accomplish for us. Of course, as we saw earlier, there's nothing wrong with bringing our personal petitions before God. We *should* do that. The problem arises when our prayers become so self-centered that we think only of our own needs.

Sometimes our requests command so much of our attention that we forget to pray for others. When we have desperate needs, it is all too easy for us to forget that others have needs as well.

When we see others struggling, in pain or in want, our hearts are often moved to do something to help. Whenever we can do something to alleviate someone's pain or meet their needs, it is our responsibility and privilege to do so. But sometimes there seems to be nothing we can do. We feel helpless.

But we should never forget that there is something we can do for them—something powerful: We can pray for them. No matter how trite "I'll pray for you" might sometimes sound to our ears, it is not a trite act if we follow through. Great power is released when we address God on behalf of another person. As James writes, "pray for each other so that you may be healed" (James 5:16).

Praying for someone is a way of loving them.

This kind of prayer is usually referred to as *intercessory* prayer. It has the wonderful benefit of enlarging our hearts toward others, as well as taking our focus off ourselves. And intercessory prayer is one of the ways God prefers to accomplish His will. He wants our prayers to be the tools He uses to bring healing, provision, and hope into the lives of others. When we intercede for others, we carry in our heart their burdens so that they need not carry them alone. Praying for someone is a way of loving them.

———

Think about the people in your life who have needs and burdens. Will you commit yourself to praying for them? Perhaps it would be good to keep a running list of prayer requests. As you find a few moments, pray for the people on your list. Then, once in a while, check in with them to see if they still need you to keep praying or if they just need the encouragement of knowing that someone is dedicated to praying for them for the long haul. I have people for whom I have been praying for many years. My regular prayers for them knit our hearts together and deepen our relationships, even when I don't see them as often as I would like. Intercessory prayer is the glue that binds us together.

13

Don't Just Talk, Listen

A common mistake we can make about prayer is to think of it primarily as monologue. We tend to consider only our part of the conversation. We talk to God, letting Him know our needs and desires. Then we close with our amen and go on our way, thinking that once we let Him know what we need that our prayers are done.

That would be fine if praying were like putting a message in a bottle and tossing it into the sea of eternity, where we hope it will reach its destination, but we never know for sure. Instead, prayer is more like a phone call or a vigorous email exchange. Two parties are involved. No true conversation takes place when only one party is speaking. It takes two people to have a conversation, and if prayer is a conversation, we ought to learn to listen as well as speak. We should not be content with filling the air with our words. We should also attune our ears to listen, for God wants to speak to His children.

All too often I have spent my time in prayer pouring out my heart to God, letting Him know of my needs and desires, of my hurts and doubts, of my confusion and pain. I have confessed my sins and thanked Him for His grace toward me. Then, I have risen from my knees and gone about my business.

How do you think your spouse or a good friend would feel if you walked up to them, gave them a complete report on the status of your life, told them what you needed from them, and then shook their hand and promptly left?

Isn't that often the way we approach God?

Because God longs to have a relationship with His children, prayer is not a formal exercise but an experience of real communication. He is not only the God who listens and hears—He is the God who speaks. If we take the time to listen closely, we will sense direction, encouragement, rebuke, guidance, or whatever it may be that He yearns to say to us.

Of course we are not listening for an audible voice. Instead, we listen for a voice that arises from the quiet depths of the heart. There is nothing weird or scary or overly mystical about learning to listen to God. It is not about "hearing voices" but about becoming attuned to His quiet inner nudgings. It is about the conviction that comes when we quiet all our restless thoughts and worries, tune out the many distractions, and just listen to what God communicates in the deep interior of our souls.

It is usually in a gentle interior whisper, rather than a thunderous voice, that God is most likely to communicate with us.

Perhaps the most important and difficult lesson we need to learn in the school of prayer is how to quiet ourselves so that we can hear His voice in the tumult of our lives. Our circumstances, our selfish desires, our fantasies and dreams, the confusing advice of others—all these can sometimes drown out the "still small voice" with which God speaks to us. It is usually in a gentle interior whisper, rather than a thunderous voice, that God is most likely to communicate with us.

Remember the Old Testament story about Elijah, who was frustrated and confused by the sins of his people and the apparent inaction of God? He had tried to speak God's word, but the people not only failed to listen, they even sought to kill him. God told Elijah to go stand on the mountain for "the LORD is about to pass by." First, Elijah was greeted with a wind so powerful that it tore rocks loose from the mountain, but "the

LORD was not in the wind." Then the ground began to shake so powerfully that he could barely stand, but once again, the Lord was not in the earthquake. Then a fire raged before his eyes, but the Lord was not in the fire. Finally, after all these powerful and showy manifestations (the kind we would associate with a supernatural occurrence) there is "a gentle whisper." When he heard it, Elijah recognized that this was how God had come to reveal Himself—a quiet, still small voice (1 Kings 19:9-13). If Elijah had not quieted himself, he never would have heard God speaking.

Perhaps this is why the psalmist recognized the need for silence. In Psalm 62:5 (NASB) he speaks to himself, "My soul, wait in silence for God only." In Psalm 46:10 we find the familiar command: "Be still, and know that I am God." Waiting upon God is one of the most important keys to transforming prayer. François Fénelon reminds us that God is always speaking to the heart that quiets itself enough to listen. "God never ceases to speak to us; but the noise of the world without, and tumult of our passions within, bewilder us, and prevent us from listening to Him." Therefore, we need to practice silence as part of our praying.

———

Quiet isn't always comfortable for us. When we quiet ourselves and everything around us, our inner chaos usually opens up and we recognize our inner turmoil. We find this so disturbing that we want to flee from it by getting busy doing something else or by filling our prayer time with our own words and requests. Instead, silence is an important preparation for prayer, a way to get ourselves ready to pray in a meaningful way and to listen for the Divine voice.

The friends I am most at ease with are the ones with whom I don't feel uncomfortable sometimes just sitting in silence together. I don't feel the usual need to fill the empty spaces with mindless chatter. So it is with God. Sometimes the most powerful prayers are those birthed in silence, just quietly anticipating that God might want to speak to me in that still, small voice.

If we were to spend time with someone who is wiser than we are, wouldn't it be a good idea to let him or her do most of the talking? And God is far wiser than even the wisest among us. We need to learn to keep quiet in order to hear Him when He speaks. Mother Teresa once said, "It is in the silence of the heart that God speaks. God is the friend of silence—we need to listen to God because it's not what we say but what He says to us and through us that matters."

So it is important for us to learn to listen as part of our prayer. Many times the hearing will change the nature of our asking, transforming what we ask for and shaping it more certainly to God's will for our lives.

We'll need God's help to teach us to listen, as it goes against many of our natural tendencies, but it is a skill I am convinced He wants us to learn. As Jesus reminds us in John 10:3-4, the sheep know the voice of their Shepherd.

Maybe we can begin to learn to practice silence by praying this prayer that A. W. Tozer prayed:

> Lord, teach me to listen. The times are noisy and my ears are weary with the thousand raucous sounds which continually assault them. Give me the spirit of the boy Samuel when he said to Thee, "Speak, for thy servant heareth." Let me hear Thee speaking in my heart. Let me get used to the sound of Thy voice, that its tones may be familiar when the sounds of the earth die away and the only sound will be the music of Thy speaking voice. Amen.

14

Learn the Power
of Praise and Worship

Recently while driving home from work, I saw a sunset that so overwhelmed me with its beauty that a spontaneous exclamation of praise just popped out of my mouth. I am trying to learn to make that kind of response a way of life. What is our natural reaction when we see a painting so marvelously executed that it speaks to something deep within us? Or when we hear a musical performance whose virtuosity takes our breath away? Or when we witness a display of athletic prowess that seems to transcend human limitations? Is not our natural response to speak with awe and wonder of the marvels we have seen, to lift up our voice and testify of their surpassing greatness?

Is it not also natural for us to speak of our love to those we care deeply about? What relationship would be considered healthy where there was no verbal communication of care, concern, appreciation, and depth of love? It does not seem right to us that our deepest feelings should go unspoken.

When our hearts overflow with affection or admiration, we need to put words to our feelings. It should be this way not only in our relationships with those around us, but also in our relationship with God. We should tell Him how we feel and honor Him for who He is. For what is greater than the wonder of His power, more heart-stirring than the beauty of His creation, more glorious than His holiness?

Praise creates the atmosphere for prayer.

There is probably no more important element of prayer than praise and worship, adoration of the God we love. It is the basis for all our other praying, for unless we recognize His greatness and our need for Him, we have little hope of meaningful prayer. That is why I believe that praise and adoration is the best way to begin a time of prayer. To do so at the outset reflects the proper relationship in which we come with all our needs and requests. Praise creates the atmosphere for prayer.

We don't offer praise and worship because God is vain and needs our affirmation. We do it because we recognize where we stand in relationship to Him, the immensity of our need, and in recognition of how big He is and how small we are. We do it because it is only right to recognize who He is and what He has done for us. It puts our lives and our needs in perspective. Which cries out more strongly—our desire for the things we pray about or our desire for God?

———

Worship is not only an action we perform in those moments when we feel moved with gratitude, but a way of living. The great English spiritual writer William Law wrote,

> Receive every day as a resurrection from death, as a new enjoyment of life; meet every rising sun with such sentiments of God's goodness, and if you had seen it, and all things, new created on your account: and under the sense of so great a blessing, let your joyful heart praise and magnify so good and glorious a Creator.

I have found that the great hymns and the best of the modern worship choruses give me some of the words I need to bring fresh expressions of honor and appreciation to God. I often find myself singing their words under my breath. And nothing beats the Psalms for giving voice to the majesty and glory of God. I love to speak aloud these poems of adoration.

O God, you are my God,
    earnestly I seek you;
my soul thirsts for you,
    my body longs for you,
in a dry and weary land
    where there is no water.
I have seen you in the sanctuary
    and beheld your power and your glory.
Because your love is better than life,
    my lips will glorify you.
I will praise you as long as I live,
    and in your name I will lift up my hands.
My soul will be satisfied as with the riches of
        foods;
    with singing lips my mouth will praise you.
                            (Psalm 63:1-5)

And there is power in praising God. Remember the story of Jehoshaphat in 2 Chronicles 20? He was a Jewish king who, by God's instruction, sent his singers into battle in front of the fighting men. By a miracle, the sound of praise and worship led to the defeat of the enemy. Perhaps there are enemies in our lives that could be defeated by the power of praise and worship. A trusting song of praise in the midst of adversity might be just the prayer that will turn things around.

15

Practice the
Presence of God

A turning point in my prayer life came when I discovered a small book titled *The Practice of the Presence of God*. It didn't contain many pages, but every one of them spoke to me about a different way to think about my prayer life. The book opened my eyes to a simple but powerful form of prayer: the usually wordless *prayer of presence*. This consists of simply placing ourselves in the presence of God and enjoying the fellowship of close intimacy with Him.

Brother Lawrence, the author of that book, was a seventeenth-century monk. He was not a widely known spiritual leader in his day. In fact, he had the unheralded job of working in the monastery kitchen. But he was a man who fervently desired a deeper relationship with God, one that went beyond the devotional acts required of him as a monk. He was not satisfied with

the occasional religious ecstasy that came through performing his required religious duties; he wanted to experience a deeper intimacy with
God. He wanted to learn to dwell
habitually in God's presence.
Eventually, his eyes were opened
to the reality that we are always in
God's presence, even when we are not aware of it. The
conclusion he reached, though, was that his awareness
and consciousness of God's presence was something
that could change his life. So, amidst the clutter and
clatter of the kitchen, while he cooked and cleaned, he
learned to experience the reality of God's presence. He
writes of that experience (speaking of himself in the third
person):

*We are always in God's
presence, even when
we are not aware of it.*

> By force of habit and by frequently calling his
> mind to the presence of God, he has developed
> such a habit that as soon as he is free from his
> external affairs, and even often while immersed
> in them, the very heart of his soul, with no effort
> on his part, is raised up above all things and stays
> suspended and held there in God.

Brother Lawrence referred often to what he called
"the interior gaze," a conscious turning of our heart and
mind toward God throughout the day. "We should
make a private chapel of our heart where we can retire

from time to time to commune with Him, peacefully, humbly, lovingly." Likely something like this is what the apostle Paul was speaking of when he encouraged believers to "pray without ceasing" (1 Thessalonians 5:17 NASB).

The psalmist wrote of recognizing God's presence in his life:

> Where can I go from your spirit?
> > Or where can I flee from your presence?
> If I ascend to heaven, you are there;
> > if I make my bed in Sheol, you are there.
> If I take the wings of the morning
> > and settle at the farthest limits of the sea,
> even there your hand shall lead me,
> > and your right hand shall hold me fast.
> > > (Psalm 139:7-10 NRSV)

God is always with us. The question for us to ponder is whether we remain aware of this truth. We can achieve this sense of God's presence by making a conscious choice to be aware of Him throughout the day. We can pray as we go about our various activities, letting prayer season everything we do. If practiced regularly, the prayer of presence becomes as natural and integral to us as drawing our next breath. It also takes the focus off what we want to get out of prayer and makes it about building our relationship with God.

There is nothing strange about practicing God's presence. It is a natural outgrowth of an intimate relationship with God. As Brother Lawrence reminds us:

> The holiest, most common, most necessary practice of the spiritual life is the presence of God, that is to take delight in and become accustomed to His divine company, speaking humbly and talking lovingly with Him at all times, at every moment, without rule or system, and especially in times of temptation, suffering, spiritual dryness, disgust, and even unfaithfulness and sin.

Such a practice is life-transforming. Brother Lawrence writes about the joy of this transformation:

> The time of business does not with me differ from the time of prayer; and in the noise and clatter of my kitchen, while several persons are at the same time calling for different things, I possess God in as great tranquility as if I were upon my knees at the blessed sacrament.

So whether I am sitting at my desk at work, playing a round of golf, sitting in the waiting room at my physician's office, taking a walk, or doing dishes (just like Lawrence), I have learned to frequently remind myself that I am in the very presence of God, and I lift my heart toward Him in wordless prayers of love and appreciation. Practicing His presence changes the way I live, it changes the way I relate to others, and it continues His work of transforming my soul.

To learn more about this practice I recommend you find a copy of Brother Lawrence's amazing little book and let this humble monk be your teacher in the school of prayer. If nothing else, maybe it will help you not to dread doing the dishes.

16

Discover the Power of Contemplative Prayer

In previous chapters we talked about listening prayer and about practicing God's presence. Both of these come together in *contemplative* prayer. Contemplative prayer brings together the intimacy with God we can experience in prayer with a deep sense of reverence for God. As James Houston suggests, contemplative prayer is one of the primary ways that intimacy with God becomes real and personal to us: "Contemplative prayer is for those who are discontented with second-hand descriptions of God and who want to experience the intimate presence of God for themselves."

Some people are uncomfortable when they hear the phrase *contemplative prayer*. They fear it is somehow connected with Eastern mysticism or New Age practices. Without question some have suggested methods of praying that seem unsound and at odds with the biblical picture of relationship with God. But a tradition of contemplative prayer has been practiced by Christians down through the ages—by Protestants, Catholics, and Orthodox alike. It is not about "becoming one with the universe" or chanting a mantra, reaching an altered state of consciousness or trying to extinguish the self and reach nirvana. In contemplative prayer we are not trying to achieve a special state of consciousness; we are trying to reach the heart of God. Contemplative prayer is all about relationship with God, about experiencing intimate communion with the One who loves us. It is about putting ourselves in a place where we can better hear and obey…and be changed by our encounter with God.

Contemplative prayer begins with what some have called "centering down." The purpose of centering down is to get our focus off all the worries and distractions of your life and onto the Lord. It is about becoming focused on the moment and being truly present where you are. For starters, you may need to consciously release the tension in your body and your mind, releasing the worry and anxiety to God. Quiet your mind. Quiet your heart. Let your cares drop away as you place them in His hands. Let Him calm the storms that rage within you and embrace the gentle silence of His peace.

One way to think about centering down is that it is like composing yourself before you give a talk in front of a group or prepare to deliver difficult news to someone. What do you do? You take a few deep breaths, you shake off the tension, you bring your mind into focus, and you breathe a prayer. You ready yourself to be completely present in the moment—all there. So it is with centering yourself in prayer.

This isn't as easy as it sounds. The moment we begin to center down, all our concerns and anxieties come rushing into our minds. It is not unlike what happens when we lie down to sleep and find ourselves assailed by all the cares of the day. At first, the attempt to compose ourselves may make us feel even more unrest within. But as this happens, we can surrender ourselves to God and choose to trust Him. The apostle Peter writes "Cast all your anxieties on him, for he cares about you" (1 Peter 5:7 RSV). It sometimes helps me to visualize myself taking each of my concerns and placing it into His hands...and leaving it there.

As I center down, I also become aware of my sin and shortcomings. This awareness provides an opportunity for confession and repentance, for a godly sorrow over all my self-justifications and excuses, and for embracing God's forgiveness and grace. It's a time for saying no to some of my desires and saying yes to the better way God has for me.

Then, as I become more centered and more fully aware, I can practice what Richard Foster calls "beholding the Lord." We are not centered so that we can become more relaxed or peaceful (though these are often wonderful by-products), but so that we can give our focus totally to the Lord with the inward gaze of our heart. Our heart looks upon Him and enjoys the warmth of His presence. Worship and adoration arise from deep within us. This is an opportunity for us to go beyond all our religious verbiage and reach out to Him in love with our whole heart and soul.

The ultimate goal of contemplative prayer is what Thomas à Kempis called "a familiar friendship with God."

At this point, we become ready to listen, to be still and listen. To hear God speak to us. Richard Foster has written so well of what this experience is like:

> At the center of our being we are hushed. The experience is more profound than mere silence or lack of words. There is a stillness to be sure, but it is a listening stillness. We feel more alive, more active, than we ever do when our minds are askew with muchness and manyness. Something deep inside

has been awakened and brought to attention. Our spirit is on tiptoe, alert and listening.

We are not listening for an audible voice or expecting some overpowering mystical experience. We are listening with our heart, not just our mind. And our heart will hear things that change us, even if we may not be able to rationally explain the changes that occur. We are transformed by the act of hearing with our heart.

What we seek in contemplative prayer is not momentary spiritual exaltation—a feeling that is wonderful but soon passes. Instead, we desire an intimate familiarity with God that teaches us to become more attentive to His gentle whispers during the course of every day. Contemplation teaches us to listen.

The ultimate goal of contemplative prayer is what Thomas à Kempis called "a familiar friendship with God." I don't think he was talking about a trivialized concept of friendship where God is our buddy. It was something bigger and more profound. Throughout the Scriptures, whenever someone came face-to-face with God, they experienced a deep and overwhelming awe. They usually found themselves on their knees, overcome by the majesty of God. The power of contemplative prayer is that it brings us into an experience that is both intimate and reverent. We are drawn close to the heart of God and begin to see Him and ourselves in a deeper and more authentic way. We begin to grasp our own smallness and pettiness, and we see the Lord in all His greatness and power and wisdom. The familiarity that Thomas spoke of is the basis for the deepest kind of friendship, where we know and are known.

17

Learn the Discipline of Dart Prayers

Sometimes I just don't have time to stop what I'm doing for an extended session of prayer. I enjoy doing that when I can, but it isn't always practical. What I *can* do is to pray lots of short prayers throughout the day—quick little bursts of prayer. During my day at work, while driving or enjoying a conversation or a TV program, sometimes aloud or sometimes just under my breath, I pray lots of short prayers to remind myself of my connection to God or to request His intervention in the many events that occur in any given day. You might think of it as twittering aimed at God—short messages to check in, to ask for assistance, or just to offer a word of thanks or praise.

Many of the saints of old practiced this discipline throughout the day, like little darts aimed toward heaven. All kinds of experiences can be the occasion for these dart prayers. Turning the corner and seeing an awe-inspiring vista of beauty can awaken praise for God's glory. The wail of a siren can remind us to pray not only for those involved in that emergency, but also for friends who need strength in a difficult time. Sitting down to a meal can remind us of what we have and bring forth a prayer of gratitude. The glimpse of a homeless person along the road is a reminder to pray for those in need (and to look for practical ways to help them).

When we get stressed out or confused or hurt by another, we can immediately request God's aid and comfort. When a friend just happens to cross our mind, that can be a signal to pray for him or her. When we look in the mirror to brush our teeth or shave, we can pray for ourselves—for forgiveness, for guidance, for help in becoming a better, kinder person. As we lie on our beds at night and the memories of the day wash over us, we can think through them with God, praying about the things that worry us and offering thanks for the many small beauties to be found in even the hardest of days. In the morning we can commit our day to Him before our feet even touch the floor.

———

Praying these dart prayers throughout the day helps prayer become not just something we do but a way of life. Praying with this frequency trains us to go to God first and to learn to depend on Him whatever may befall us, whether good or bad. These prayers keep us connected to the Lord.

If we are paying attention, every day provides hundreds of reminders to awaken us to the need for prayer and to keep us praying. If you've never prayed this way before, try it for just one

Praying these dart prayers throughout the day helps prayer become not just something we do but a way of life.

day. Stop often to shoot a prayer heavenward for needs that you become aware of, when you feel thankful or grateful, or on behalf of the people you meet that day. If you find it hard to remember to pray throughout your day, you might set your watch for every half hour as a reminder. Or wear some jewelry that prompts you to pray every time you see it. You might even tie a string around your finger!

The goal is to learn to bathe each day in prayer, to let prayer wash over your life and fill it with joy and intimacy with God. Perhaps by doing this we come as close as is reasonably possible to praying without ceasing. You'll find that these frequent reconnections with God will change the way you experience your day.

18

Pray with Others

From much of what we have discussed in this book, you might conclude that prayer is a personal and private matter. And yes, sometimes it is. Much of your time in prayer will be just between you and God. But if you are praying only by yourself you are missing an important element of prayer. My life has been so enriched by praying *with* other people, seeking the Lord and lifting up our needs together. Somehow the prayers prayed with someone else always feel a little more powerful.

Prayer is not meant to be practiced only in private. It is also a communal practice, meant to be engaged in with others. Jesus said, "Again, I tell you that if two of you on earth agree about anything you ask for, it will be done for you by my Father in heaven. For where two or three come together in my name, there am I with him" (Matthew 18:19-20). Jesus saw prayer as an activity that would bind believers together as they seek to bring the power of God to bear on the issues that face us not only as individuals but as members of a congregation, a city, a state, a nation, and the world. God loves to work in concert with the multiplied prayers of His people. When our voices are raised together in prayer, things happen!

That is why nearly every church service includes a time of prayer. But I don't think that a few minutes of shared prayer during worship is really enough. If we want to experience the full joy and power that can be found in praying for one another, of hearts and voices being joined in supplication and intercession to God, we'll need to make room for more opportunities to pray with others than merely during the Sunday service.

———

It is unfortunate that many believers today have largely lost sight of the need to pray together. I can remember a time when most churches had a weekly prayer meeting, a time when people could gather together as members of a Christian community to pray for each other's needs and the needs of the world. Perhaps the rarity of prayer meetings today is a sign of the decline in our understanding about prayer and in our passion for praying. Probably most churches have ceased to have regular prayer meetings because they believe no one will show up. And many Christians, if they were honest, might admit that the idea

of spending an hour in prayer is
almost unimaginable. It sounds
so boring. But prayer meetings
can be anything but boring. They
can be a wonderful way to draw
believers together, enriching the
sense of community and of being

*God loves to
work in concert with
the multiplied prayers
of His people.*

on a spiritual journey together. You might want to consider starting a prayer meeting in your church. Here are
a few thoughts about how to make it work:

Make it easy for people to get involved. You might
start with meeting just once a month, thereby help-
ing people ease into the idea of getting involved. If you
think it would be hard to get people to pray for an
hour, start with half an hour. You might even hold the
prayer meeting just before a worship service. That way
people don't have to commit to an extra trip to church,
plus it helps set a nice tone for the worship experience
when you know people have been praying in advance
of the service.

*Explain what you are going to do so that people feel less
intimidated.* Most people think that it would be hard
to sit quietly and pray (or listen to the long-winded
prayers of others). So it is helpful to explain the struc-
ture of a normal prayer meeting, which usually involves
sharing needs aloud and spreading the responsibility
of praying among a number of people. Explain that

there will be time for discussion of needs, times for praying aloud together, and times for individual silent prayers. Spending time sharing requests helps make for more specific prayers, aimed at specific needs. Specific praying is so much more exciting and meaningful than mumbling together about generalities and making unfocused requests for "blessing." If you can, get everyone involved. Try to spread the prayer requests around so that no one monopolizes the time with their prayer soliloquies.

Hold the meeting in a comfortable location. No need to make this an experience in asceticism. Stress the naturalness and adventure of prayer by exploring together some of the varieties of prayer we have discussed in this book. You might consider an occasional experiment in praying through a passage of Scripture together. If you create a sense of community and purposefulness, people are much more likely to make it a habit.

In addition to group meetings for prayer, many have found it helpful to have a "prayer partner," someone with whom they can regularly pray and share requests. Whether you meet over coffee every week or two, pray over the phone, or just exchange prayer-filled emails, it is important to have someone in your life that you can share times of prayer with. It is not essential—or maybe even advisable—that this person be your best friend. Sometimes it's easier to share more vulnerable requests with someone who is not so intimately involved with your life. The other advantage to partnering with someone who is not one of your closest friends is that your times together will more likely be centered on praying rather than just engaging in the conversations you would otherwise fall into with a best friend. Seek out a mature Christian with whom you can build a relationship for the express purpose of praying together. Of course you'll want to find someone whose spiritual outlook is essentially the same as yours so that prayer times don't digress into disagreements about the mechanics and theology of prayer.

Whether with a special prayer partner, as part of a prayer group or prayer meeting, or just in the normal Sunday services, it is important to not let praying become an entirely private matter. We need the support and focus and encouragement that others can give us in prayer, and praying together helps cement our sense of being part of a supernatural community—the body of Christ.

19

Use a Variety of Spontaneous and Written Prayers

When it comes to romance, there is nothing like a beautiful poem or a "mix tape" of favorite love songs to express yourself to the person you adore. Sometimes a poem or song so aptly and beautifully expresses the deepest sentiments for which you just can't find the right words. And for the one who receives them, knowing that you chose these words as an expression of your passion makes them a gift to be treasured as though they came from your own mouth or pen.

Similarly, we should not be afraid to use the words of others as guides in our praying. Praying written prayers can be a wonderful addition to your life of prayer. Of course, it would be unfortunate if we *only* prayed the prayers written by others, for it is also good for God to hear the fumbling expressions of our own hearts, no matter how unpoetic they might be.

He treasures them as if they were the most beautiful and powerful prayers of the greatest saint. Just as the beloved always longs to hear us say a simple "I love you," so God loves to hear our most imperfect prayers. But it doesn't have to be an either/or. The healthy prayer life can include both spontaneous prayers from the heart and carefully constructed prayers written by others.

———

Many Christians labor under the false idea that the only true and authentic prayers are spontaneous and extemporaneous. But where did such an idea ever come from? The Scriptures themselves offer numerous models of prayer, such as the Lord's Prayer and the Psalms. There is a psalm to fit just about any emotional state we find ourselves in. And the Lord's Prayer was given in response to the disciples' request that Jesus teach them how to pray. These scriptural prayers, as well as prayers found in collections such as *The Book of Common Prayer*, can give us the words we need to say what needs to be said. They can become guides to help our prayers be complete, and they allow us to focus on the intent of our prayers rather than getting caught up in composing them.

Praying a prayer written by someone else is like reciting one of Shakespeare's sonnets to someone you love—we express our feelings using Shakespeare's words.

We invest them with our own emotions and let them give voice to things we feel so deeply but may not always know how to express. Written prayers can give us words to frame our thoughts and feelings and help us pray beyond our limitations or fixations. They remind us to pray

Write out a prayer to God as you would write a love letter.

about things that might otherwise slip our mind. And they give us phrases which we can use to more perfectly express our own feelings. In the appendix you'll find a small collection of some of my favorite prayers. I hope some of them will become favorites for you.

I've found for myself that a balanced diet of prayer includes both extemporaneous cries from the heart and the discipline of written prayers. Sometimes I'll sit down and compose my own prayers to God, just as one might compose a poem. I encourage you to write out a prayer to God as you would write a love letter. Work and rework it until it says just what you want it to say. Then offer it to God—a prayer composed with diligence and heart and depth of expression. You might even want to share it with others.

Also, you might want to invest in a good collection of written prayers that you can offer up to God.

There are many good books of prayers available. Sample them until you find one that expresses the thoughts you'd like to express. Then pray them slowly, thinking about every word and truly making them your own. You'll find that your personal prayer vocabulary will be expanded and strengthened...and it might just add a little more poetry to your prayers.

20

Expose Yourself to What Inspires You to Pray

One of my favorite places to pray is along a deserted beach on the Oregon coast. Sometimes I will make the hour-long drive there just so I can walk along the beach, watch the waves lap onto the shore and the seagulls wheel in the sky above me, and feel the sand between my toes. I'll often find an old piece of driftwood and use it as a walking stick as I venture far up the shoreline from where I parked, just walking and talking with God. It is a place both quiet and beautiful. I find my soul calmed and am better able to focus on what really matters. It clears my mind and opens me up for listening to God whisper into my heart.

It is a place both quiet and beautiful, and it clears my mind and opens me up for listening to God whisper into my heart.

Another good place for me to pray is on a hike through the woods, following a winding path among the trees and vegetation. There it is quiet, except for the song of birds and the occasional sound of a squirrel scurrying about in the underbrush. As the sunlight slants down through the trees, I can see the dance of dust motes in the clearing. Here I feel my human smallness in the face of nature, but I also find it to be a place where intimacy with God comes easy. Here my heart seems naturally lifted to praise.

———

But it isn't just the beauty of nature that inspires me to pray. Another great place for me is an art museum, where the beauty and ingenuity of artistic masterworks somehow lift me above my earthly cares and pry my heart open with real vulnerability. A visit to the Metropolitan in New York, the Art Institute of Chicago, the Kimball Museum of Art in Fort Worth, Texas, or even a small local exhibition of paintings often gives me an experience like visiting a great cathedral. The wondrous human achievements of aesthetic beauty are echoes of a divine artist I feel drawn to in the midst of all this glory.

The work of spiritual poets such as Gerard Manley Hopkins, T.S. Eliot, William Wordsworth, John Donne, George Herbert, Mary Oliver, and Wendell

Berry can be another spur to prayer for me. Many of
their poems are either meditations on transcendent
realities or actually take the form of prayers. I find myself wanting to unearth my inner poetry to express
thanks to my Creator.

And music. Ah, yes, music. I am lifted out of my
worries and struggles by the heartrending beauty of a
Bach concerto, a symphony by Mozart, or a glorious
cantata by Handel. Or perhaps, in a different mood, it
will be the jazz of John Coltrane, a world-weary Johnny
Cash lament, or the poetic lyrics of Bob Dylan that will
move me deeply and make me feel as if I am in the presence of the One who sang the world into existence.

These are just a few of the things that always seem
to put me in the mood for prayer. If you think about it
for a minute or two, you could probably name some of
your own: a stirring worship service, sitting on a bench
and watching children play in the park, a long walk in
your neighborhood, or maybe a drive in the country.

Of course we can't always be running off to the
woods or the ocean or an art museum whenever we feel
the need to pray. Our busy lives don't permit that. And
besides, it isn't necessary to have the perfect conditions
to experience a precious time of prayer. We need to
also learn how to pray at the most inconvenient times

and in the most inhospitable places. But it is always a good idea to occasionally give ourselves the opportunity to go somewhere that inspires us or to engage in some activity that increases our desire for fellowship with God.

Whatever it may be that ignites your desire to pray, make room for it. If you find it hard to find the time, then schedule it in as a divine appointment—your personal place to meet with God.

21

Pray the Scriptures, Especially the Psalms

It hasn't always been true for me, but I have learned to love reading the Bible. Not because I'm a super saint (just ask the folks who know me), but because of the effect it has on my life. In it I find nourishment for my soul, guidance for my daily life, challenge to my self-centered way of living, and comfort for those times when I need it most. It has proven so important to my spiritual life that I have made it a habit to read the Bible every day.

A few years ago, someone introduced me to a way of reading the Bible that saints throughout the ages have used to feast upon the riches in God's Word. It's called *lectio divina*, which is Latin for "divine reading." If that sounds forbidding or difficult, don't worry. The medieval monks used it as a way to pray, but it is just as easy and relevant for you and me today.

In this kind of reading, you read much more slowly
than you normally would, and as you read you turn
each verse, each phrase—sometimes even each word—
into a guide for praying. Although you can easily read
a couple of chapters in as little as five or ten minutes,
in *lectio* you sometimes spend five or ten minutes to
move through a single verse. It isn't meant to replace
normal reading and study, which are also important,
but it offers a different experience in Bible reading—
one aimed at personal application. I have found that
it makes the Bible come alive for me in a practical and
life-transforming way. And it provides power and scriptural guidance for my prayer life.

———

Here's how it works. You choose a passage and read
through it slowly (for me it often helps to read it aloud).
As you read you pause over each phrase and let yourself
be guided in prayer by that phrase. Some have called it
pray-reading, because each phrase has the potential to
summon up a whole host of things you can pray about.
You may find yourself asking God to make the promises in the verse a reality in your life, asking Him to
reveal how you might better live out its teachings, con-
fessing how you have fallen short in this area, or praising God for what it reveals about His majesty.

Try it out. Just pick a passage and read it slowly.

Pause and reflect, then pray—pray its truths into your heart and mind, using the Bible as a personal love letter from God, offering hope and challenge and instruction. "In *lectio divina*," writes Richard Foster, "we are doing more than reading words, we are listening with the heart to the Holy within. We are pondering all things in our heart as Mary did. We are entering into the reality of which the words speak, rather than merely analyzing them."

> *Pause and reflect, then pray—pray its truths into your heart and mind.*

As you begin this practice, I think you will find that almost any passage of Scripture will provide plenty of touch points for prayer.

Another way to experience the power of the Bible in your prayers is through praying the book of Psalms. Throughout the history of the church, the Psalms have been known as the prayer book of the Bible. This Old Testament book contains 150 songs, poems, and prayers that Christians hold dear. Most churches in the liturgical traditions include a reading from the Psalms in every worship service. Many phrases from the Psalms have found their way into lovely hymns, both ancient and new, into popular worship choruses, and even into rock songs by bands such as U2. Poets have echoed and reflected the beauty and power of the Psalms in their lyrical creations.

Because the Psalms use parallelism rather than rhyme as their poetic device, they translate beautifully into any language. And untold millions of believers have turned to the pages of the Psalms for hope and inspiration during dark times. The famous Twenty-third Psalm is one of the most well-known and oft-memorized pieces of writing in all literature. I learned it as a child and still recite it sometimes in the face of fear and uncertainty. It never fails to give me hope and strength.

The reason the Psalms continue to be such a popular book is that they give words to the full range of human emotions. I don't think there is any human emotion that doesn't find expression somewhere among this collection of poetic writing. The Psalms are given to us to make our own, to reflect our needs and desires and struggles. They provide words for emotions that are sometimes beyond our ability to express, giving shape to our shapeless feelings and intuitions.

Often the Psalms provide words we can make our own in offering praise and worship to God. Many of them recognize the power of the almighty Creator, the one whose holy beauty is reflected in the wonder of His creation. With the Psalms I lift my heart in acknowledgment of God's greatness.

At other times, the Psalms reflect the injustice of life and the confusion that overwhelms us from time to time, making honest declarations about the struggles we all face. In their honesty the Psalms even record the outbursts of anger toward God that the psalmist felt when everything around him seemed to be going wrong and God seemed distant and uncaring. With the Psalms I find permission to be honest and open toward God, even engaging in arguments that, though I know I will not win, perhaps need to be vocalized so that He can show me a better way.

Sometimes the Psalms offer words of great comfort for our darkest hours, times when fear and dread overtake us, when we are mourning the loss of something or someone dear to us, or when we are confused about the seeming absence of God in the midst of the pain. In the Psalms I find the hope to go on, the faith to believe, and the comfort and assurance of knowing that He is always with me.

———

The mysterious power of the Psalms can be found in the paradox of their nature. They are raw and uncensored expressions of the wide range of our experiences, offered to us as the prayers of fallible human beings. But at the same time they are also beautiful words of hope and restoration and conviction that arise from those who knew God intimately and had experienced His love and mercy firsthand. The divine and the human are wedded together in the words of the Psalms.

In the Psalms God has given us language that we can use in our conversations with Him. Often, when we just don't have the language to speak what is in our hearts, we'll find in the Psalms the right words to express what we are feeling—whether thanksgiving, awe, fear, anger, loneliness, uncertainty, or love. At other times, a reading of the Psalms will uncover feelings and emotions we weren't even aware were within us.

Whether you are praying one of the Psalms or slowly and meditatively praying over a passage of Scripture, you'll find that the Bible is not only our greatest resource for learning to pray, but a tool that can help us pray prayers that are life-changing. You'll discover that praying Scripture will broaden the scope of your prayers and reveal new areas that need God's intervention and grace in your life.

22

Accept the Mystery of Unanswered Prayer... and Keep Praying

Sometimes we experience miraculous immediate answers to our prayers.

Other times, the answers unfold slowly, like a flower in the springtime.

And there are still other times when our prayers seem unheard—when we do not get what we have so passionately requested. All of us know the disappointment of fervent prayer that fails to produce the prayed-for result. It can be confusing and painful. It can cause us to doubt the efficacy of prayer, our relationship with God, or even His goodness. Unanswered prayer is one of the great troubling realities for every Christian.

But there is really no such thing as an unanswered prayer. Our prayers are always answered. God's ear is always attuned to our requests, but sometimes His answer is not the one we wanted. There are three answers given to prayer: yes, no, and wait.

Sometimes our prayers are not answered because we are selfish and ask for things that wouldn't be good for us. "When you ask, you do not receive, because you ask with wrong motives, that you may spend what you get on your pleasures" (James 4:3).

> There are three answers given to prayer: yes, no, and wait.

Sometimes our prayers are not answered because God has a bigger plan in mind. When the apostle John makes a promise about answered prayer, it comes with a caveat—that it be the will of God. "This is the confidence we have in approaching God: that if we ask anything according to his will, he hears us" (1 John 5:14). So if we are praying for something that is outside God's will, we won't get the answer we are hoping to receive—and thank God for that! Don't forget that even Jesus had to deal with unanswered prayer. Although He asked that the cup of death would pass Him by, He still had to go to the cross.

Sometimes we realize only in hindsight that the answer we had hoped for was premature or would not have been the best thing for us. God, in His wisdom and love, often withholds our requests on the ground that they would be harmful to our ultimate good. I am grateful that not all of my prayers have been answered in the time and the way I prayed for. "We pray for silver, but God often gives us gold instead," Martin Luther said. In retrospect I realize that some of my prayers were misguided.

Or sometimes it is just a matter of timing. Our prayers seem unanswered because we are impatient, because we do not realize that God's timetable is not the same as ours. Charles Spurgeon wrote: "Frequently the richest answers are not the speediest...A prayer may be all the longer on its voyage because it is bringing us a heavier freight of blessing. Delayed answers are not only trials of faith, but they give us an opportunity of honoring God by our steadfast confidence in Him."

———

Whatever the reasons for our unanswered prayers, we can still become discouraged about the efficacy of prayer and this can keep us from praying. Perhaps the biggest stumbling block for many people is the sense that prayer just doesn't really work. We all can probably point to times when we prayed with fervency, but it didn't seem to have any effect. Now, if our prayers are focused on obtaining the latest model BMW or a new vacation home on Cape Cod, then the lack of heavenly response would not be a surprise. But more troubling are those prayers for perfectly commendable needs that don't seem to get much of a hearing from God. Sometimes we don't get what we *want*; sometimes it seems like we don't get what we *need* either. When all our unanswered prayers are multiplied together, it may leave us with a sense of fatalism about praying. Why bother?

Maybe we can understand if He doesn't fulfill our self-centered requests, but what about the prayers for a suffering child or a friend facing a painful illness? Or someone whose burden could be eased by a little bit of money miraculously appearing in their checking account? These are harder for us to understand. And unless we have closed our eyes to reality, we know that prayers for even the bare sustenance of millions of Christians living in crushing poverty around the world appear to be going unanswered. What do we do with all this?

I have no satisfying answers to the questions about why God sometimes works miracles, but sometimes doesn't. The best I can do is suggest that since He is not a machine or a system we can manipulate, that He operates as He wills. That He sees a bigger picture. That, of course, doesn't make all my questions go away. Prayer is still something of a mystery.

So why pray at all? First, because prayer is more

about living out our relationship with God than it is about getting answers to specific needs and desires. Second, because God has invited us to pray, and we would be foolish to miss out on such an invitation. And third, because God loves to partner with human beings to accomplish His will in the world and sometimes amazing things do happen when we pray. Our prayers are one of the main tools for that partnership. As Blaise Pascal suggested, "God has instituted prayer so as to confer upon his creatures the dignity of causality." Likewise, Charles Spurgeon called prayer "one of the necessary wheels of the machinery of providence." Yes, one of the mysteries of prayer is that God uses it to get things done. When we pray, we come alongside God to work with Him, to be given a taste of participation in the continuing act of creation. As Abraham Heschel wrote, "To pray is to dream in league with God."

When our prayers are not answered the way we think they should, we need to remember the wisdom of God, the One who sees the bigger picture, who has a perspective that we could never see. We have to accept that prayer is not a magic formula and that sometimes God chooses not to answer our prayers despite our best motives and intentions. Sometimes it just makes no sense to us. And this side of eternity, we may never be satisfied with why some prayers seem to go unanswered. But *seem* is the key word here, for in truth God hears our every prayer. He listens. He cherishes the prayers of His children.

There is no fully satisfactory answer to the problem of unanswered prayer. We will always be puzzled by why some prayers seem to work and others don't. It's a mystery we just have to accept if we are to be people of prayer. And we cannot let it discourage us from praying. Despite the questions and complications of prayer, we simply must decide to keep on praying.

23

Use Distractions to
Deepen Your Prayers

Have you ever struggled with staying focused
when you pray? I think most of us have. Do your
prayers ever go something like this: "Heavenly Father,
I thank You for Your love...*Oh rats, I need to clean out
the refrigerator. It is getting kinda smelly...um...oh yes...*
I want to pray for my sister-in-law who is worrying
about a possible diagnosis of cancer...*I wonder what
that little bump on the side of my neck might be...could it
possibly be cancer? I don't feel sick but you never know...
I wonder what my out-of-pocket costs would be if I had a
long hospital stay? Did I remember to set the TV to record
that show about doctors that I like so much...I wonder
what's on TV right now?...oh yeah,* dear God...um...*I
really need to get a haircut. Maybe I could squeeze one in
tomorrow right after work. Oh yeah, I am supposed to be
praying.* Now, what was I saying, God?"

So often, when we quiet ourselves to pray, all the distractions of our lives come crowding in. They buzz around our brain like annoying mosquitoes. Maybe the first lesson we can learn from this is that we probably don't spend enough time being quiet. We are always so busy, rushing here and there, frantically trying to accomplish as much as we can…and perhaps afraid of having to come face-to-face with ourselves if we actually quiet down for a few moments. So, of course, the floodgates are opened when we try to pray, and all the stuff we haven't thought about because we were so busy doing comes crashing in on us. Maybe if we spent more time in quiet contemplation and meditation, more time in thinking through our lives, we wouldn't have all the random thoughts come flooding into our mind every time we tried to pray.

The best thing to do with distractions is to make them the friend of our prayer time rather than its enemy.

Let's consider that phrase for just a moment: *thinking through our lives.* Perhaps one helpful definition of prayer is thinking with God about our lives. Whether we do it aloud or quietly in our heart, it's a good idea to think through our lives in concert with God. I find that whenever I need to make a hard decision, it is always helpful to get the perspective of a trusted friend. My friends frequently see things about my life that I miss. How much more valuable to get God's perspective? And how are we going to hear the gentle voice within us unless we quiet ourselves and listen?

———

Perhaps the best thing to do with distractions is to make them the friend of our prayer time rather than its enemy. I have learned to use distractions as a guide to what and how to pray. When the distraction arises, I use it as a prompt to pray about whatever it is that's distracting me: something I am worried about, a relationship that needs attention, a reason to ask or give forgiveness. If I have a piece of paper handy, I will even jot down a note to follow up on what comes to mind, and then return to the prayer at hand. Sometimes the distractions may even guide me to more important things to pray about than the ones I'm praying for.

Another thing that helps me is to pray out loud. Praying aloud, even if just under my breath, helps keep me focused. There is nothing wrong with silent prayer, but a prayer prayed aloud keeps my brain engaged better than a silent prayer.

So, as you pray, don't let your distractions discourage you. Use them as prompts to expand the scope of your prayers and as a sign of other things you might need to be praying about. If your mind goes wandering down a path, follow it with prayer. Then the distractions can become a way to strengthen your prayer life rather than making you feel defeated.

24

Learn to Become
More Awake and Aware

Earlier today, one of the women I work with stepped into my office to ask me a question and stopped midsentence, staring through the opened blinds at an Indian summer afternoon. The blue sky was intense and nearly cloudless against a line of evergreens on the distant hills, and nearby trees had burst into furiously flaming reds, oranges, and yellows. "Wow," she said, "you have such a beautiful view out your window."

When I turned to look, I felt an intense stab from somewhere deep inside. "Yes," I agreed, "it is amazingly beautiful." But I realized that in the last several days, while this gorgeous landscape from the hand of the Divine painter was being retouched with autumn fire, I hadn't even noticed.

The week had been busy and more than a little stressful. There was plenty to distract me from the wonder just outside my window. I was behind in answering some important emails, had important papers that needed to be read and commented upon, a couple of minor crises to navigate...you know, just a normal busy week. I had been too busy to pay attention. And the loss was mine. If my coworker hadn't pointed out what was just outside my window, I might have gone several more weeks without paying attention, and by then the leaves would have begun to lose their grip and to perform their slow pirouette to ground below.

A life of prayer teaches us to keep awake and notice things.

We miss so much by not paying attention.

One of the wondrous gifts that comes through pursuing a life of prayer is that it teaches us to keep awake and notice things. When we make praying a central activity of our lives, it makes a difference. For when we pursue communion and communication with God, we move just a bit closer to experiencing life through His eyes. We will be changed as we gain new perspectives and see the deep meanings that surround us every minute of every day. When we pray we come awake—awake to God, awake to ourselves, and awake to the world around us and to all whose lives intersect our own.

When I see life through God's eyes by walking

through my days with Him as my companion, I begin to pay attention. I notice the hurt in the eyes of a friend or coworker. I hear the urgent cry of a distant siren and know that someone's life is being impacted by some tragedy. I become aware of my self-centeredness and all the little lies I foist upon myself and then upon the world. I tear up with gratefulness at sweet moments of beauty and feel my heart lifted.

Open your heart to the world and bring it before God in prayer.

And all of these things become incitements to pray, to connect with the One who cares more deeply about these things than I ever could. He is also the One who sometimes uses my feeble prayers as the instrument to begin a change for the better— a healing of heart, body, or spirit, an intervention of grace, forgiveness, or protection, a deepened sense of appreciation and thankfulness that softens and transforms.

When we understand that the God who authored everything around us wants to use our prayers, we will want to be awake and aware so that our prayers can play their mysterious role in setting things right.

So, as you go about your day, stay mindful of that still small voice within. Keep your eyes open to all the beauty and hurt and longing that surround you. Open your heart to the world and bring it before God in prayer. Live the adventure of being awake by conversing with God about all that you see and experience. You might have to shake yourself awake on occasion and stare out the window to remind yourself of what you might be missing.

25

Become Open to Being the Answer to Your Prayers

A few days ago I awoke with the strong impression that I needed to pray for a friend I hadn't talked with in quite a while. I have learned to obey such urges, so I took a few minutes before climbing out of bed to ask God to be with my friend, to give him whatever strength and comfort he might need, and to watch over him. Then I rubbed my eyes and got started on my day.

Later in the day, remembering the prayer, I looked up my friend and asked him how he was doing. After receiving the usual response of "fine," I paused a moment, looked him in the eyes, and said, "No, really. Are you okay?" He was silent for a moment, looked down, and answered, "No. I'm having a hard time. A really, really hard time." So I settled down in a chair opposite him and listened as he poured out his heart about all the things that were going wrong and had driven him to wonder if life was worth living. I listened, I shared a few thoughts about similar strug-gles I had faced in my life, and offered a few words of comfort and advice.

> I am learning that the impulse to pray is often a signal for me to act.

When I got up to leave, he told me that God must have sent me because much of what I said was exactly what he needed to hear. Hours later he emailed to express again his appreciation for my thoughts, but mostly to thank me for being a friend.

I could easily have felt that offering a prayer that morning had fulfilled my responsibilities. It's easy for me to pray about something and then think my job is done. Or worse, to simply offer to pray ("I'll pray for you about that…") and think I have done my duty.

I am learning that the impulse to pray is often a sig-nal for me to act. Prayer and action should go hand in hand.

———

It is not uncommon for me to discover that God wants to use me as part of the answer to some of my prayers. As William Booth, the founder of the Salvation Army, once said, "Work as if everything depended upon work and pray as if everything depended upon prayer." The two work in harmony.

When I see a homeless person on the street, I often feel a twinge of compassion and an urge to pray—that God will meet his needs, provide him with food and shelter, and help him find his way to a better life. And it is a good thing to pray for the homeless. But might it also be that God is calling me to get involved in making a long-term difference in the lives of homeless people in my community?

When I see the starving children from across the world on my television, I am usually inspired to pray for them—that they will not only find food, medicine, and a safe place to sleep, but that they will also find a better future. But might God also be calling for me to use my time and money to help make their lives a little better?

The answer, of course, is yes. God wants us not only to pray for them, but to make a difference through our time, our money, and our votes. Our prayers and actions work together, for often God wants us to be part of the answer for the prayers we are praying. Prayer is not just a passive activity. It is, in words and actions, the act of partnering with God to fulfill His will upon the earth. We dare not use the phrase "I prayed about it" as an excuse for inactivity. Sometimes our actions give feet to our prayers.

———————

In God's eyes, our obedient and sacrificial actions are, in themselves, a form of prayer. Nicholas Grou wrote, "Every action performed in the sight of God because it is the will of God, and in the manner that God wills, is a prayer, and indeed a better prayer than could be made in words at such times."

When prayers and actions are joined together, it changes the way we live. It makes our lives themselves into a prayer. So let's not reduce our prayers to words alone; rather, let's make the totality of our lives a living, breathing prayer to God. When we see a need, it is never out of place to start with prayer. But then we should ask ourselves how God might want to use us as part of the answer.

The Life-Changing
Adventure of Prayer

Prayer is such a big and expansive topic that a little book such as this can barely scratch the surface. I hope it has helped you to think more deeply about prayer, has given you more confidence in praying, and has challenged you to explore how prayer can change your life.

An active life of prayer keeps us plugged into the power that comes from God, and it offers us the promise of spiritual growth, holiness, and a deeper intimacy with God. We must not think of it, however, as a cure-all, an escape hatch from the troubles of life, or a way to guarantee our personal happiness. Prayer is so much bigger than that. It is a work we must commit ourselves to if we are to make sense of our lives in the light of eternity. As Abraham Heschel writes,

> Prayer is no panacea, no substitute for action. It is, rather, like a beam thrown from a flashlight

before us into the darkness. It is in this light that we grope, stumble, and climb, discover where we stand, what surrounds us, and the course which we should choose. Prayer makes visible the right, and reveals what is hampering and false. In its radiance, we behold the worth of our efforts, the range of our hopes, and the meaning of our deeds.

This is why prayer, though sometimes difficult and mysterious, is so important. You'll never fully understand it this side of eternity. At times it will puzzle and perplex you. But at other times it will strengthen, guide, comfort, and surprise you. And it might change you well beyond your expectations.

Sometimes when I pray, my situation is changed. But more often when I pray, I am changed.

A Little Collection
of Prayers

My Lord God, I have no idea where I am going.
I do not see the road ahead of me. I cannot know
for certain where it will end. Nor do I really know
myself, and the fact that I think I am following
Your will does not mean that I am actually doing
so. But I believe that the desire to please You does
in fact please You. And I hope that I will never
do anything apart from that desire. And I know
that if I do this You will lead me by the right road,
though I may know nothing about it. Therefore
I will trust You always though I may seem to be
lost and in the shadow of death. I will not fear for
You are ever with me, and You will never leave me
to face my perils alone.

—THOMAS MERTON

O most merciful Redeemer, friend,
    and brother,

May we know Thee more clearly,
Love Thee more dearly,
And follow Thee more nearly,
Day by day. Amen.

—RICHARD OF CHICHESTER

O God, early in the morning I cry to You. Help me to pray and to concentrate my thoughts on You. I cannot do this alone.

—DIETRICH BONHOEFFER

Almighty God, unto whom all hearts are open, all desires known, and from whom no secrets are hid; cleanse the thoughts of our hearts by the inspiration of Thy Holy Spirit, that we may perfectly love Thee, and worthily magnify Thy holy Name; through Christ our Lord. Amen.

—*THE BOOK OF COMMON PRAYER*

Lord, make me an instrument of Your peace;
Where there is hatred, let me sow love;
Where there is injury, pardon;
Where there is doubt, faith;
Where there is despair, hope;
Where there is darkness, light;
And where there is sadness, joy.

O Divine Master, grant that I may not
    so much seek
To be consoled, as to console;
To be understood, as to understand;
To be loved, as to love.
For it is in giving that we receive,
It is in pardoning that we are pardoned,
And it is in dying that we are born to eternal life.

    —FRANCIS OF ASSISI

Most merciful God, order my day so that I may
know what You want me to do, and then help
me to do it. Let me not be elated by success or
depressed by failure. I only want to take pleasure
in what pleases You, and only to grieve at what
displeases You. For the sake of Your love I would
willingly forgo all temporal comforts. May all the
joys in which You have no part weary me. May
all the work that You do not prompt be tedious
to me. Let my thoughts frequently turn to You,
patient without grumbling, cheerful without self-
indulgence, contrite without dejection, and seri-
ous without solemnity. Let me hold You in awe
without feeling terrified of You, and let me be an
example to others without any trace of pride.

    —THOMAS AQUINAS

We receive everything from Your hand, Lord Jesus. Your powerful hand stretches forth and turns worldly wisdom into holy folly. Your gentle hand opens and offers the gift of inner peace. If ever it seems that Your reach is shortened, it is only to increase our faith and trust, that we may reach out to You. And if ever it seems that Your hand is with-held from us, we know that it is only to conceal the eternal blessing You have promised—that we may yearn for that blessing even more fervently.

—Søren Kierkegaard

Lord, open our eyes, that we may see You in our
    brothers and sisters.
Lord, open our ears, that we may hear the cries
    of the hungry, the cold, the frightened, the
    oppressed.
Lord, open our hearts, that we may love each
    other as You love us.
Renew in us Your Spirit, Lord, free us and make
    us one.

—Mother Teresa

Thou hast given so much to me
Give one thing more—a grateful heart:
Not thankful when it pleaseth me.
As if Thy blessings had spare days,

But such a heart whose Pulse may be Thy Praise.

—GEORGE HERBERT

Lord, end my winter, and let my spring begin. I cannot with all my longing raise my soul out of her death and dullness, but all things are possible with Thee. I need celestial influences, the clear shinings of Thy love, the beams of Thy grace, the light of Thy countenance. I suffer much from sin and temptation, these are my wintry signs…Lord, work wonders in me, and for me.

—CHARLES SPURGEON

Lord, I know not what I ought to ask of You. You only know what I need. You know me better than I know myself. O Father, give to Your child what he himself knows not how to ask. Teach me to pray. Pray Yourself in me.

—FRANÇOIS FÉNELON

The One-Minute Bible Guide

Terry Glaspey

Getting the most out of Bible reading time just got easier. This handy guide is small in size but big on information. Author Terry Glaspey addresses the top questions people have about the Bible, presents a 90-day reading plan, and eases the intimidation factor as he shares

- verses for comfort, peace, and grace
- seven ways Scripture helps us know God
- a five-minute synopsis of the entire Bible
- eight tools to get the most out of each reading
- one-page summaries of each book of the Bible

For avid Bible readers or those curious about the bestselling book of all time, this portable resource opens up the wonder, power, and message of the Bible.